Henry Moore's
Sheep Sketchbook

Comments by Henry Moore
and Kenneth Clark

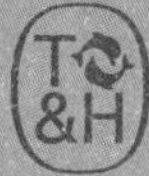

Publisher's note

The leaves are numbered as in the original sketchbook and
reproduced at their original size. By agreement with the artist,
a narrow white border has been added in order to allow the binder
to trim the edges, and as a result of the normal slight irregularities
of the binding process this may appear as a thin white line at the
edge of some pages.

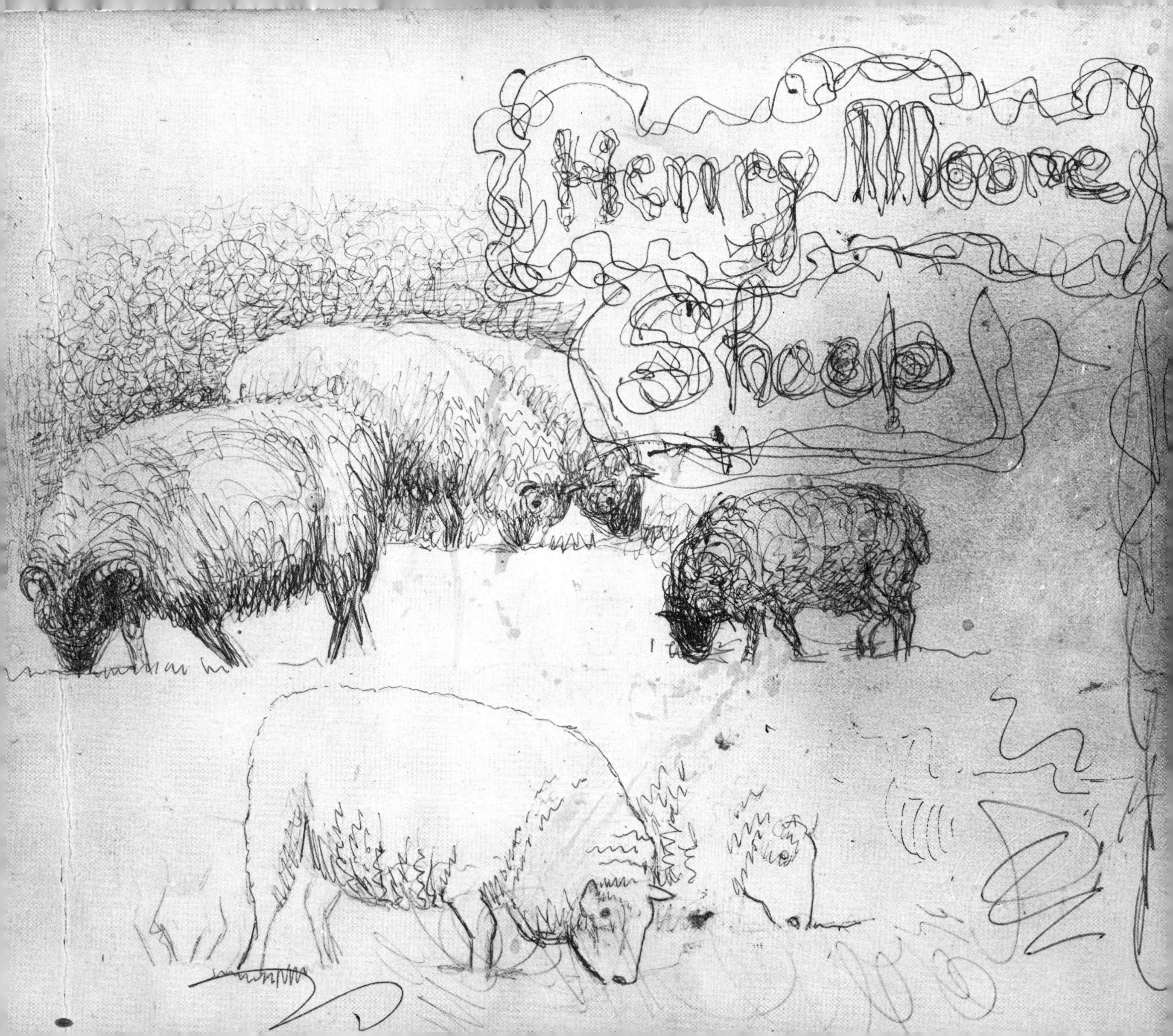

Henry Moore
Sheep

For Mary. from Dad

7th March 1972

Subjects — insects.

Tadpoles.

Sheep.

Birds.

Labyrinth.

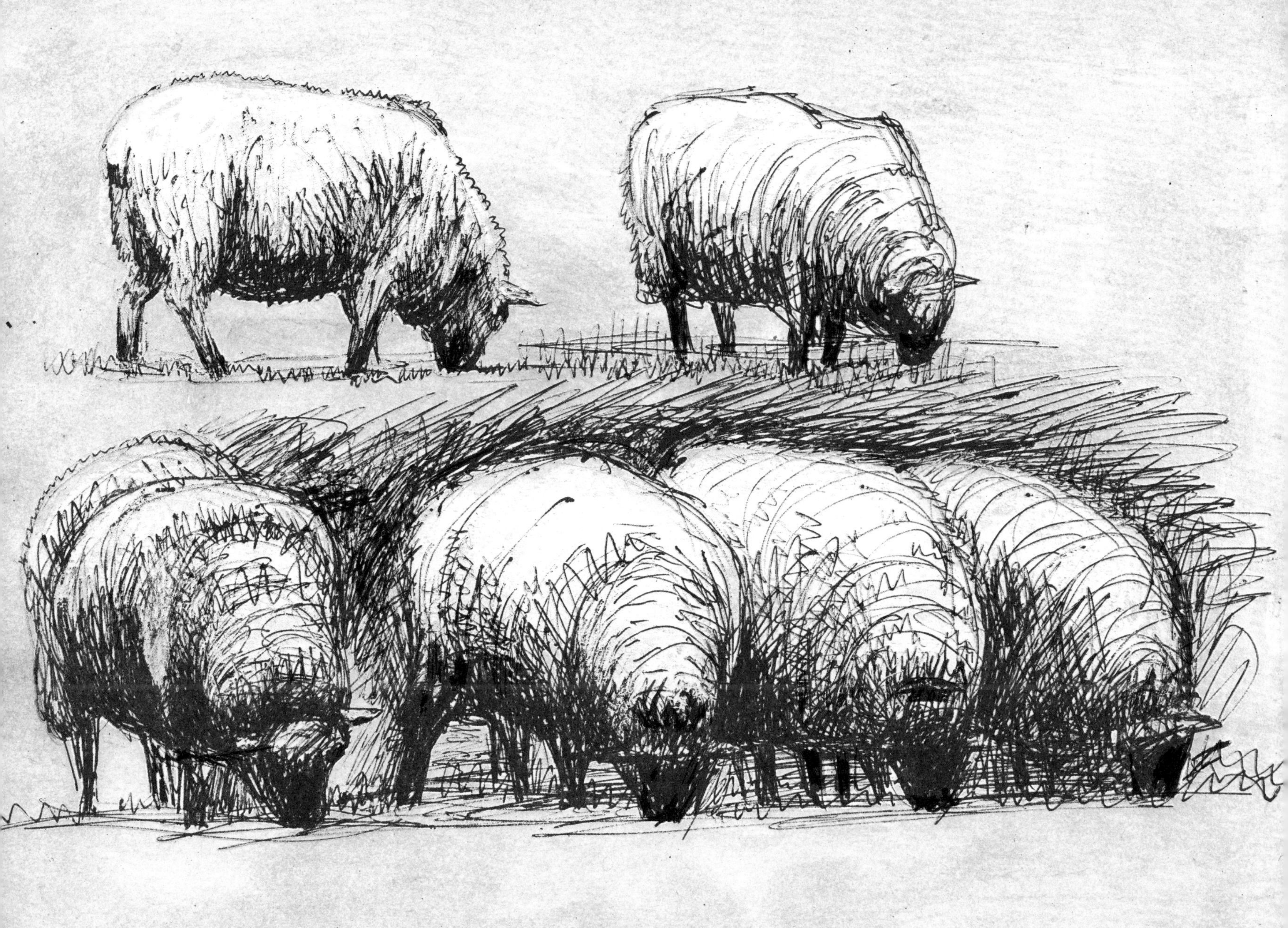

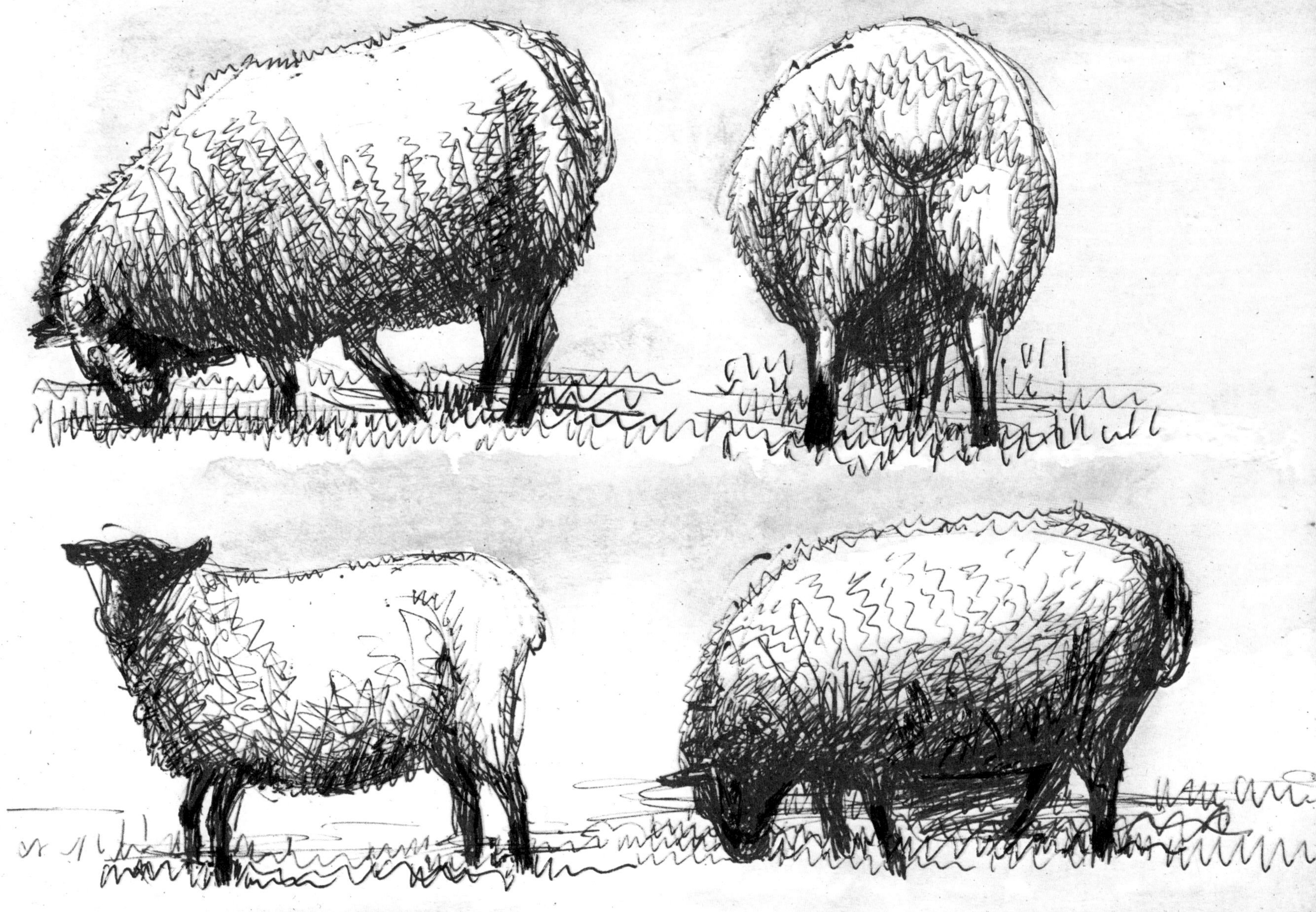

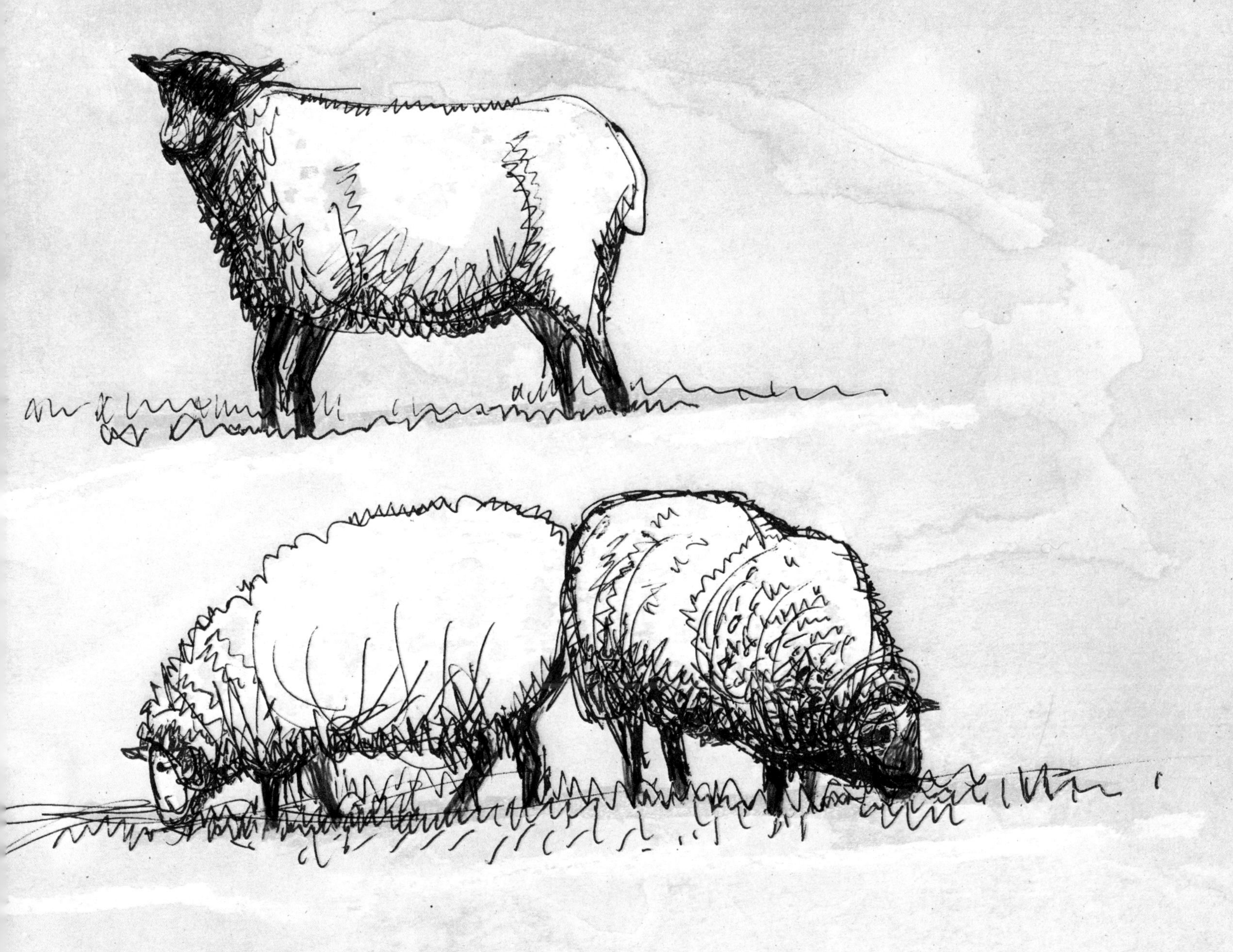

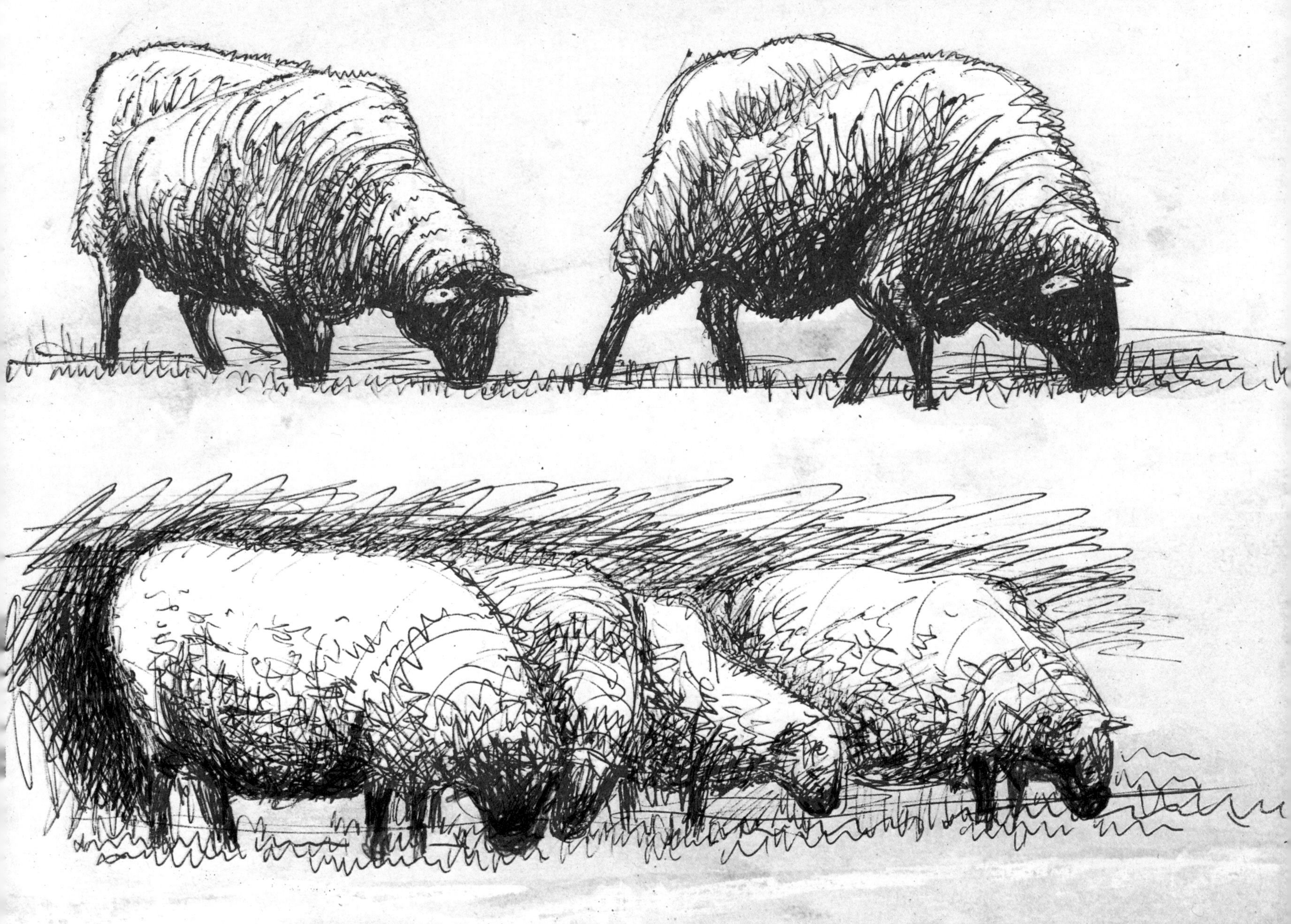

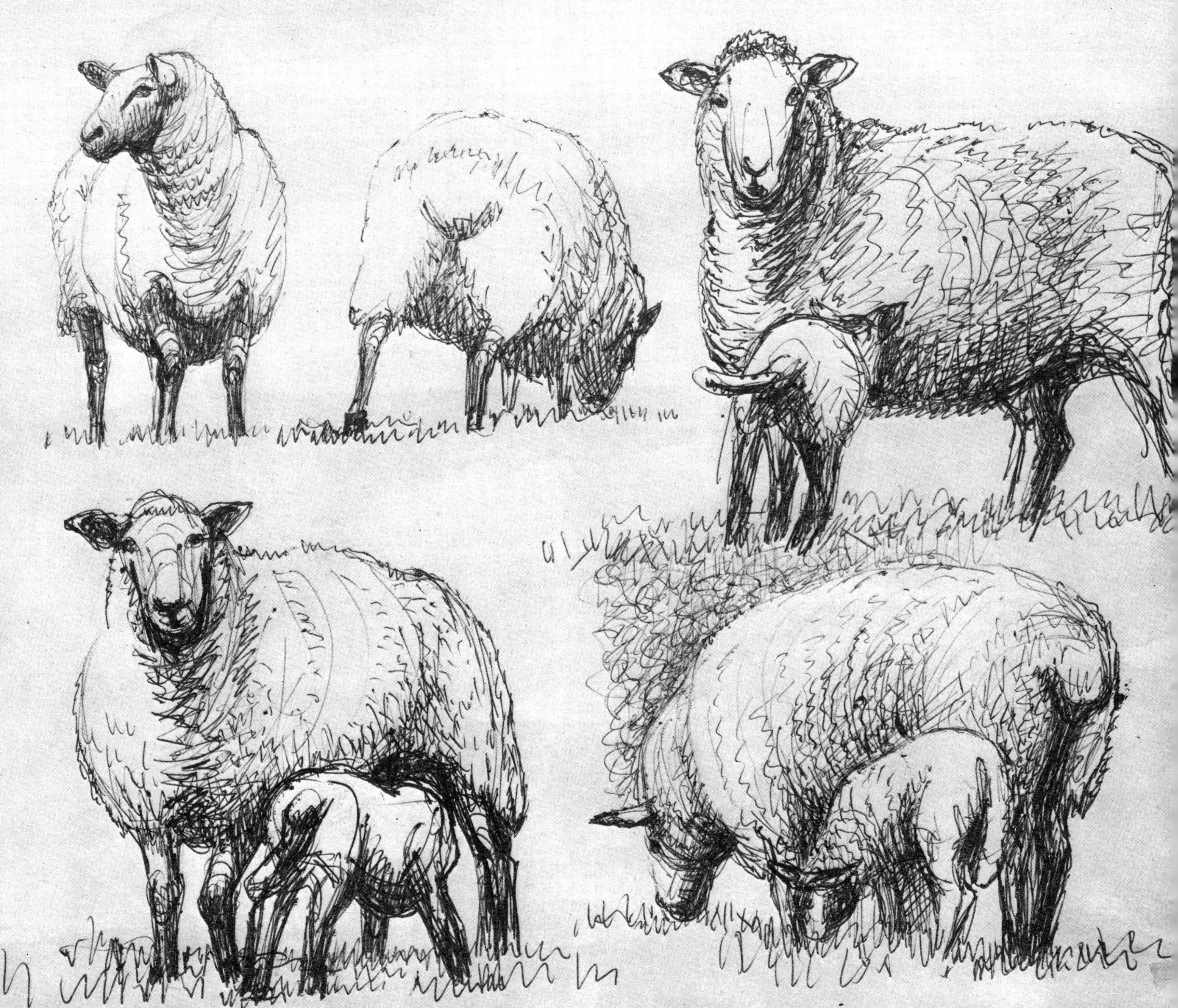

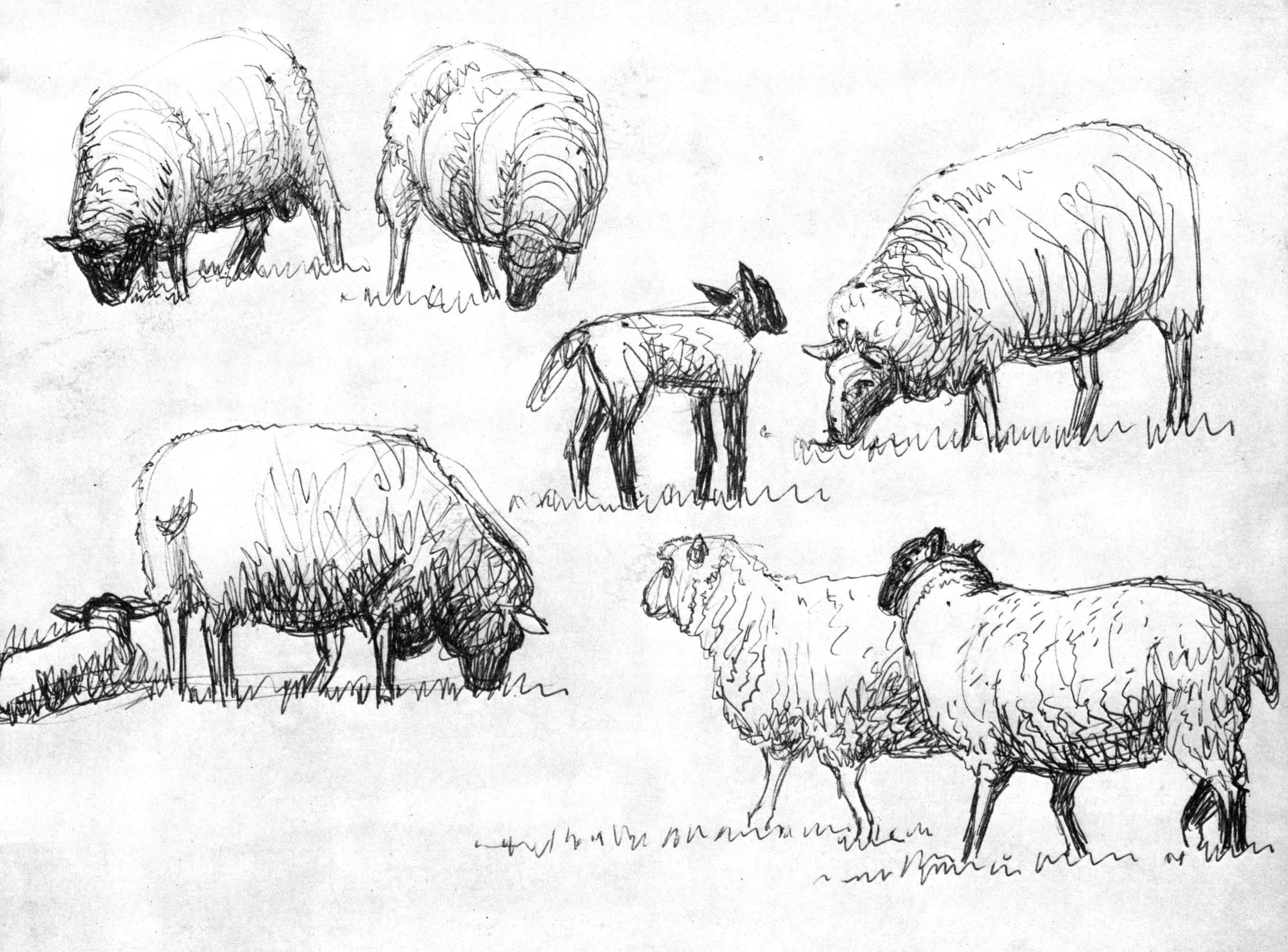

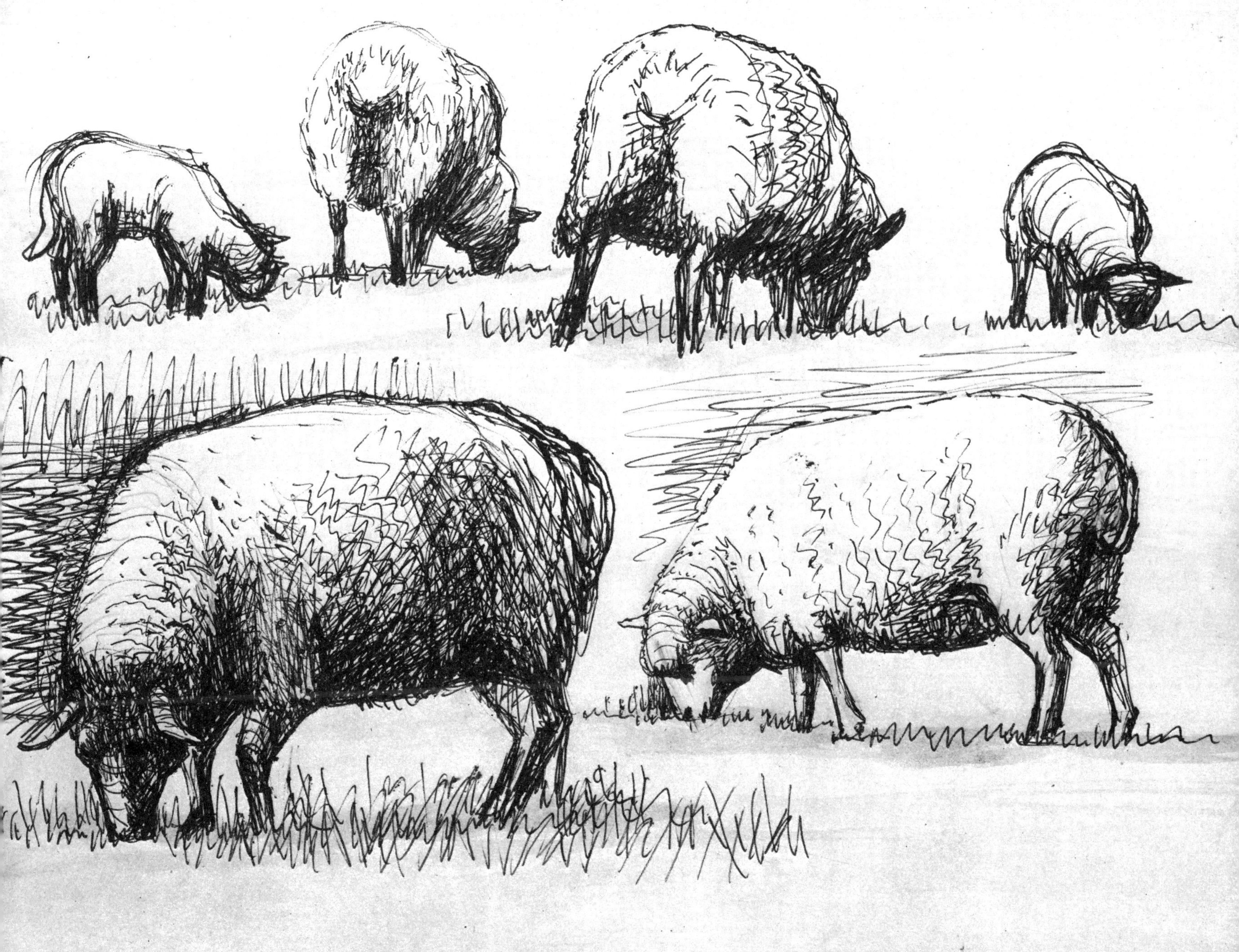

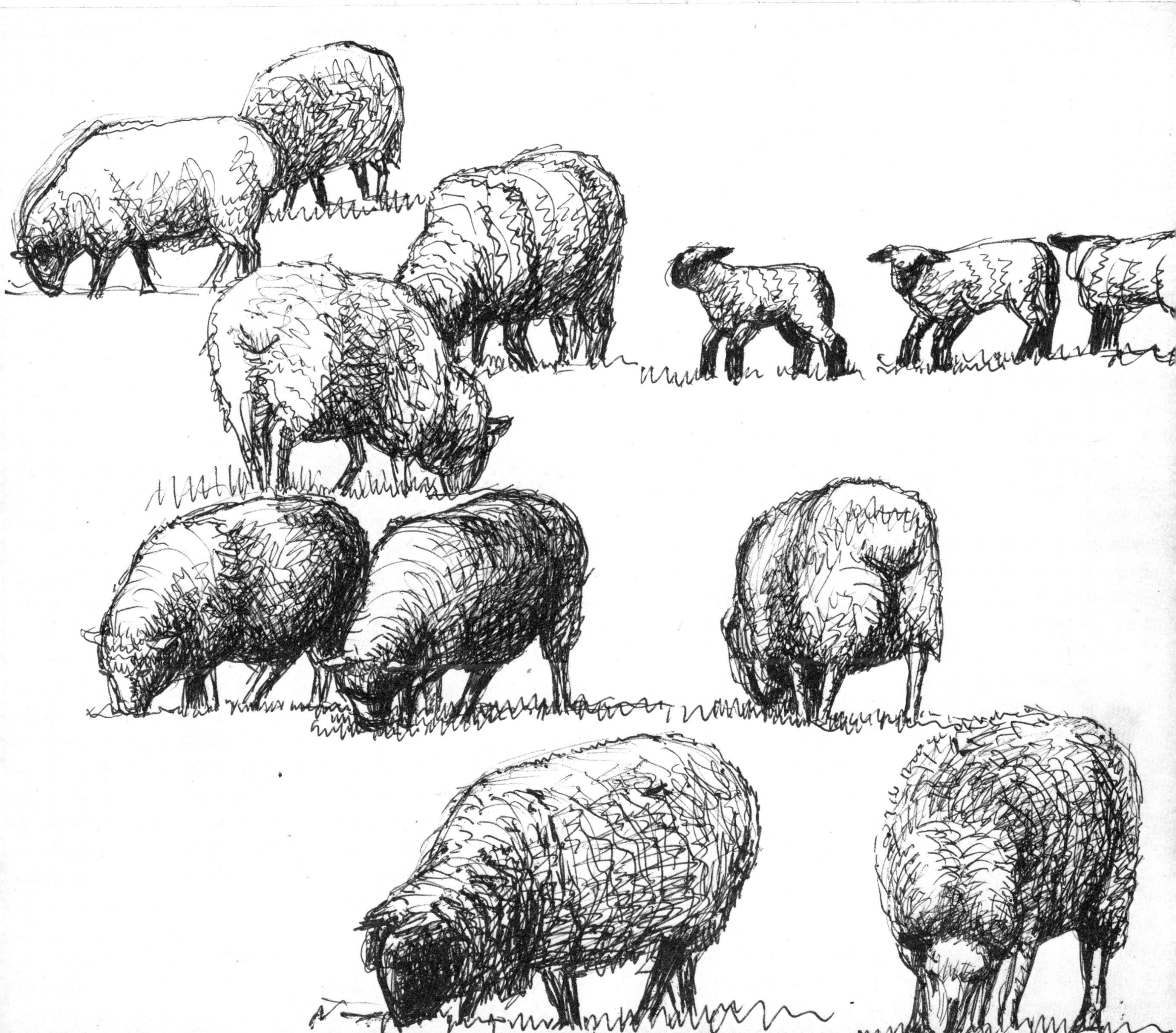

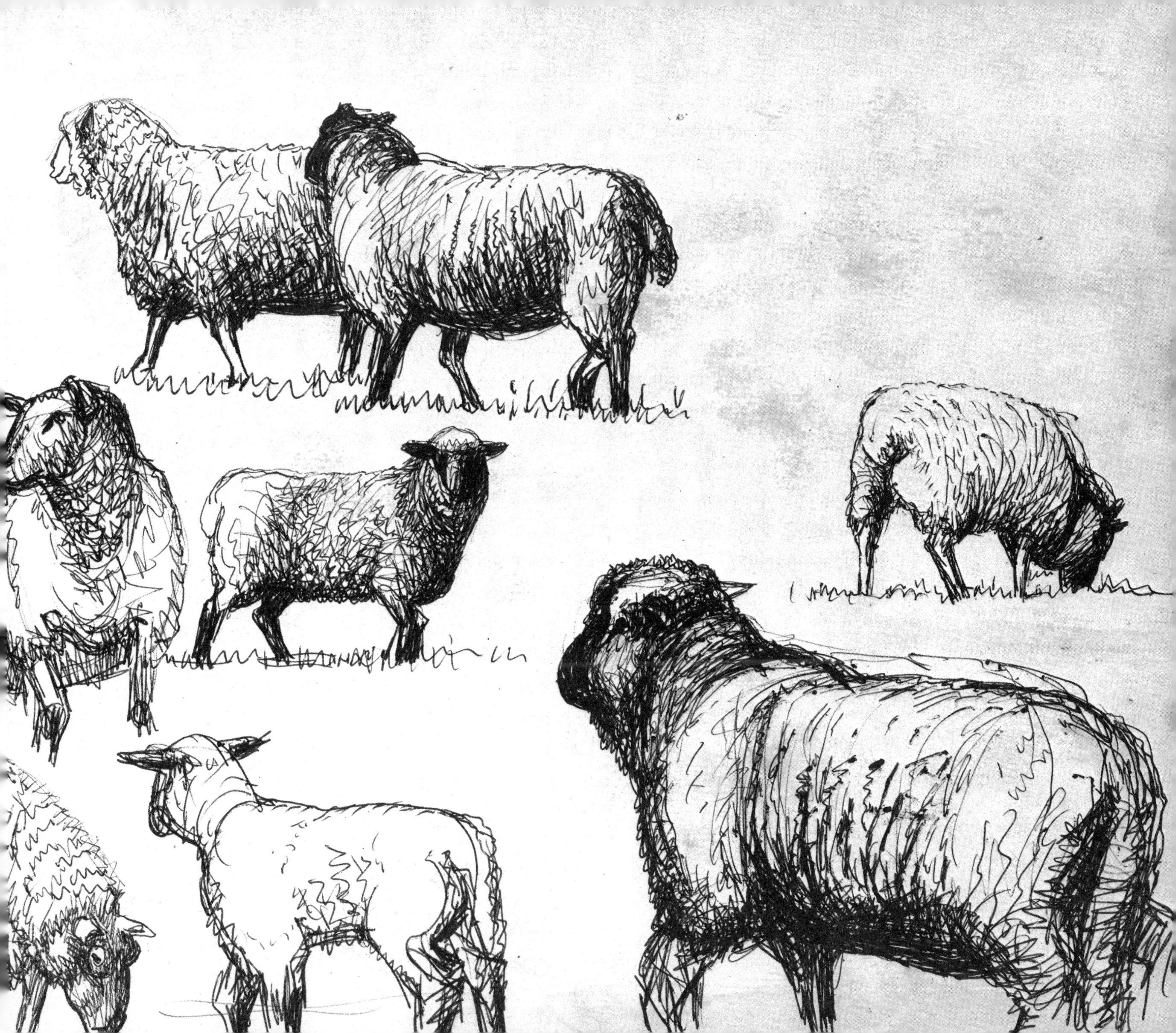

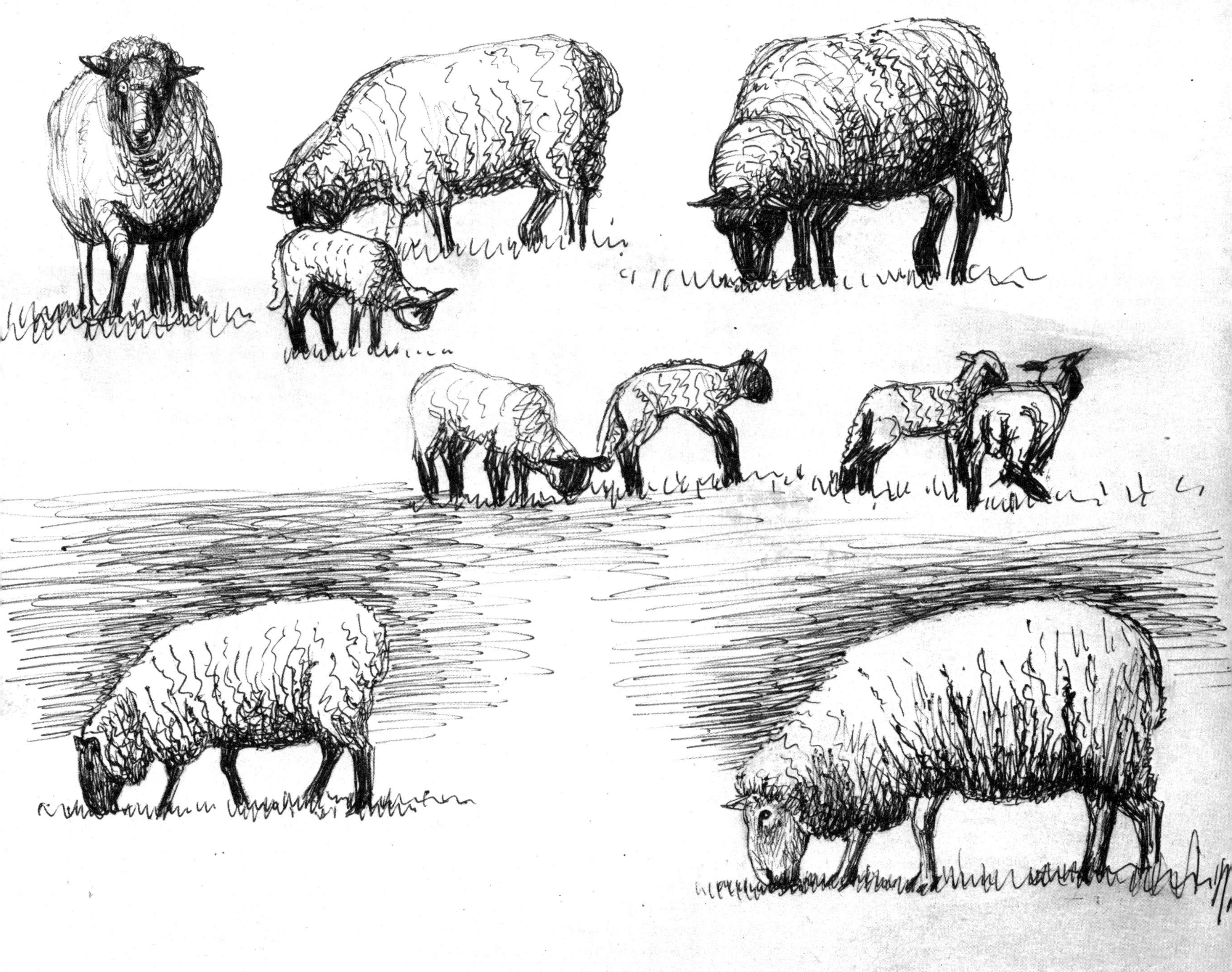

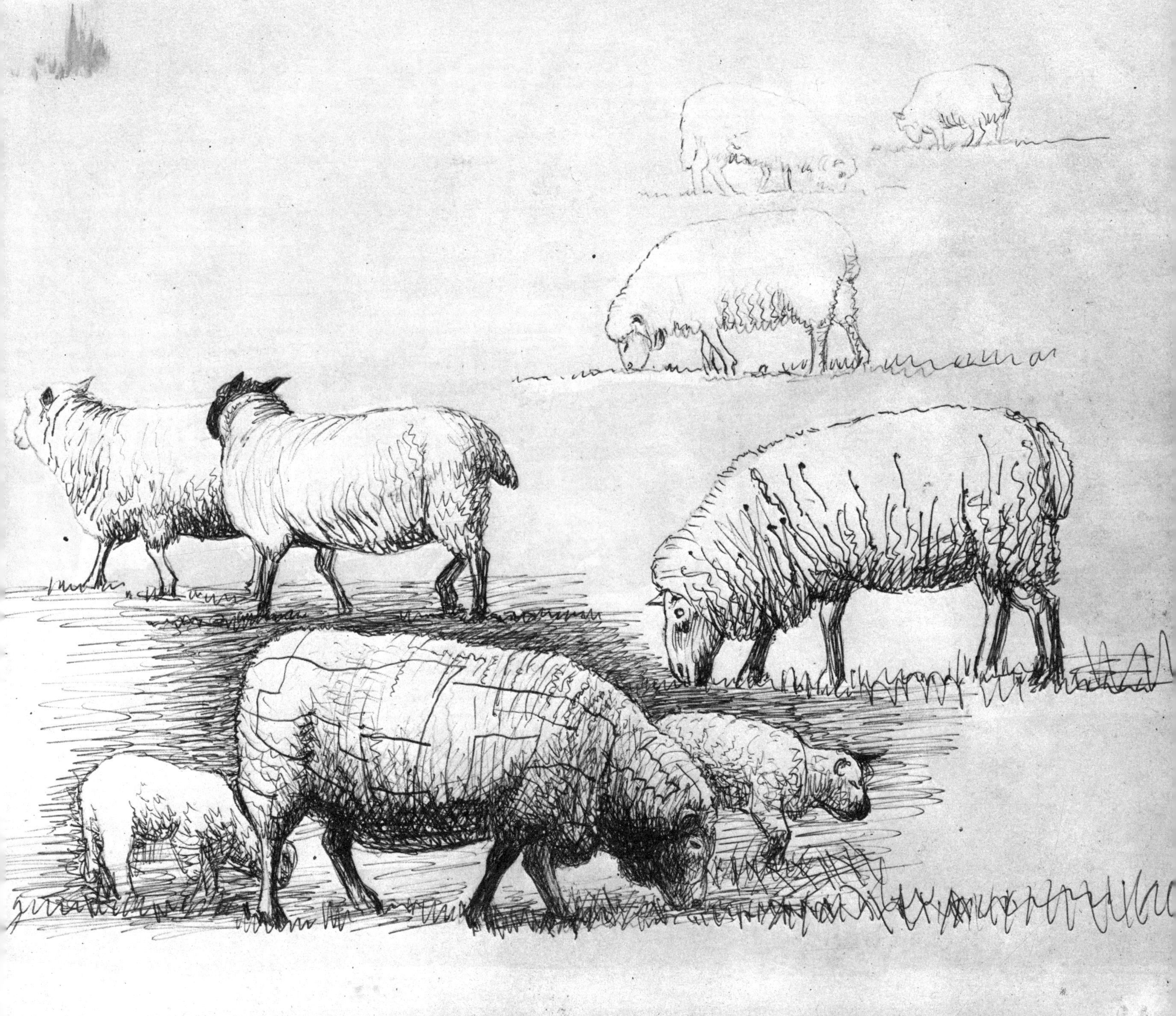

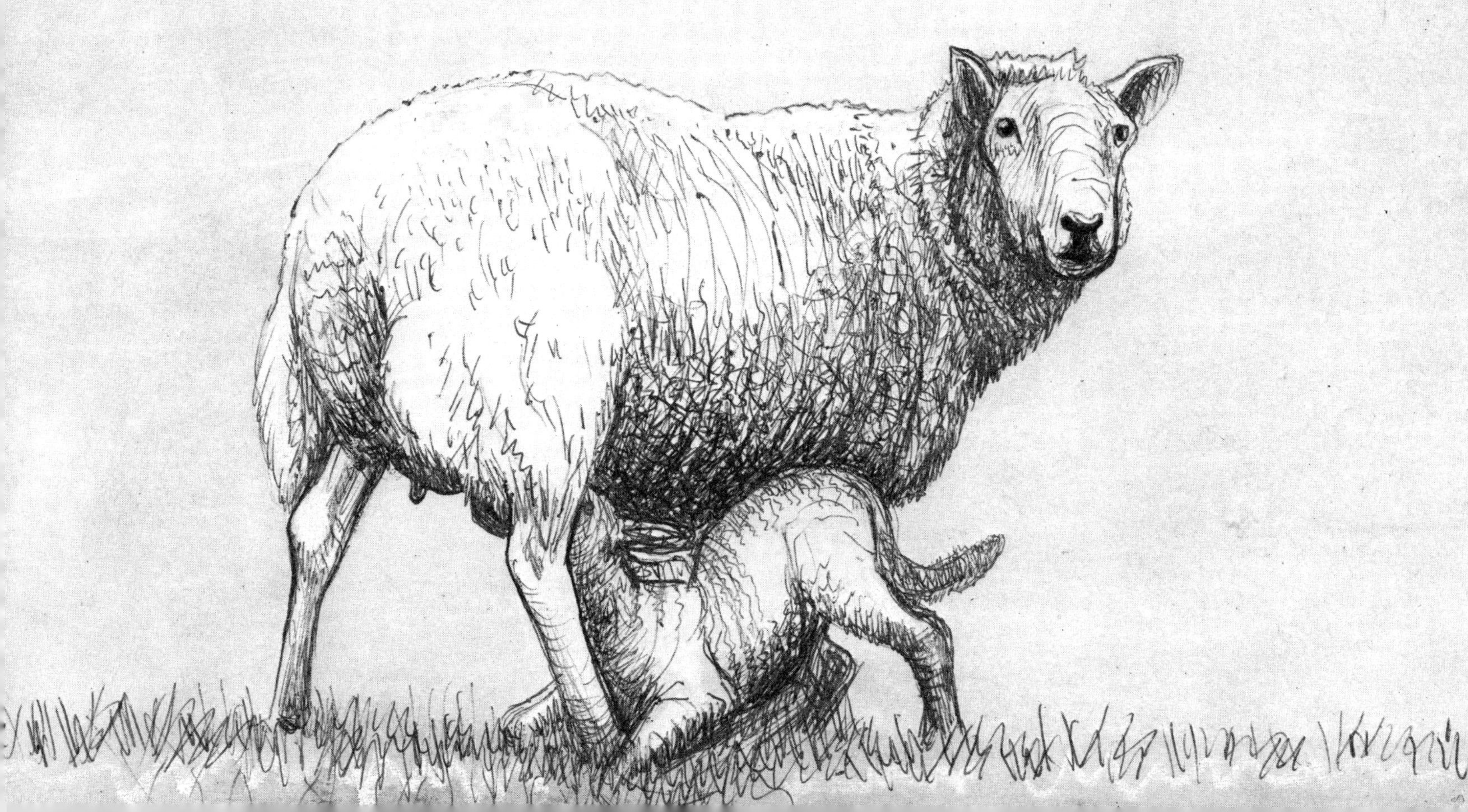

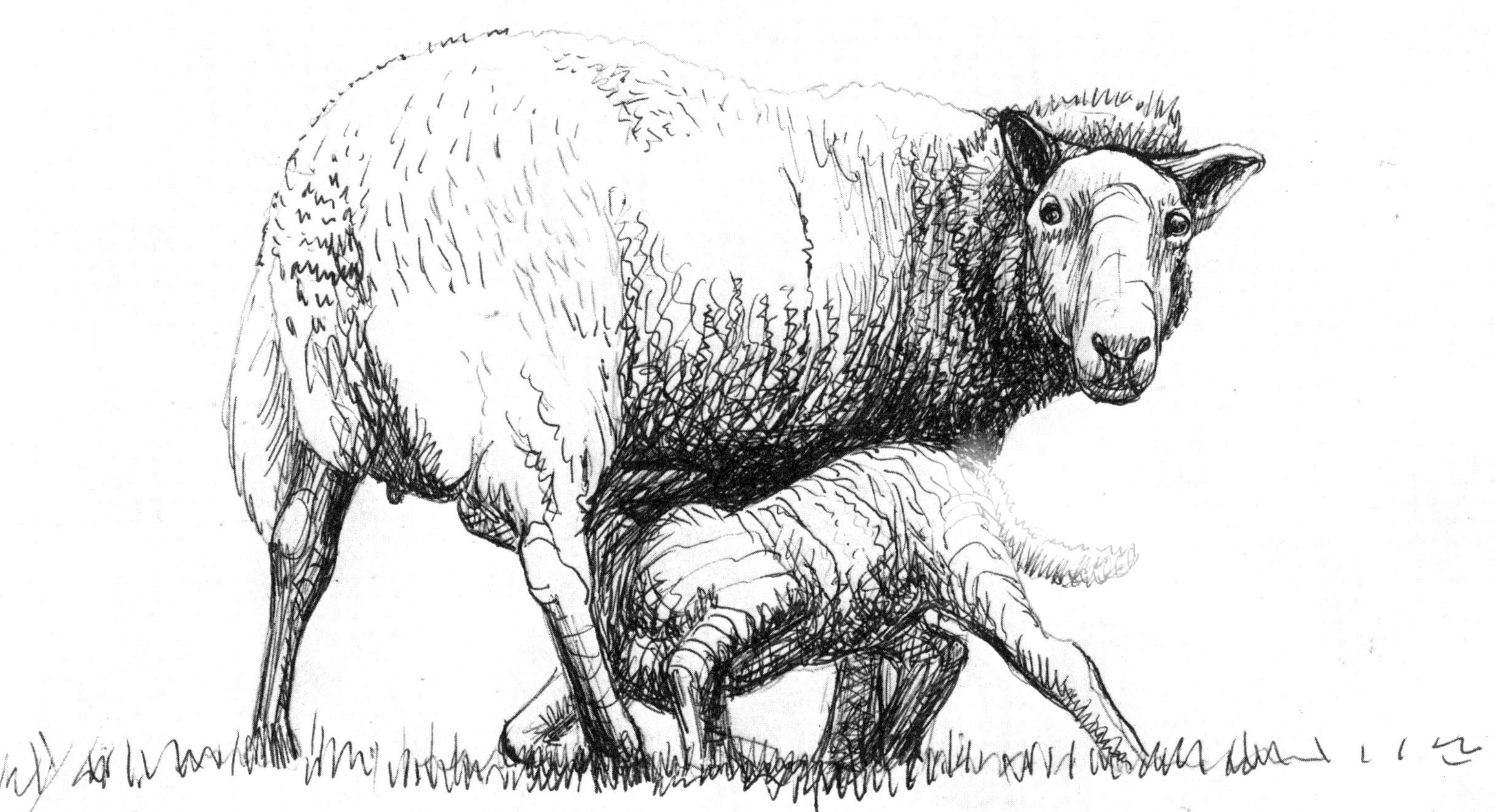

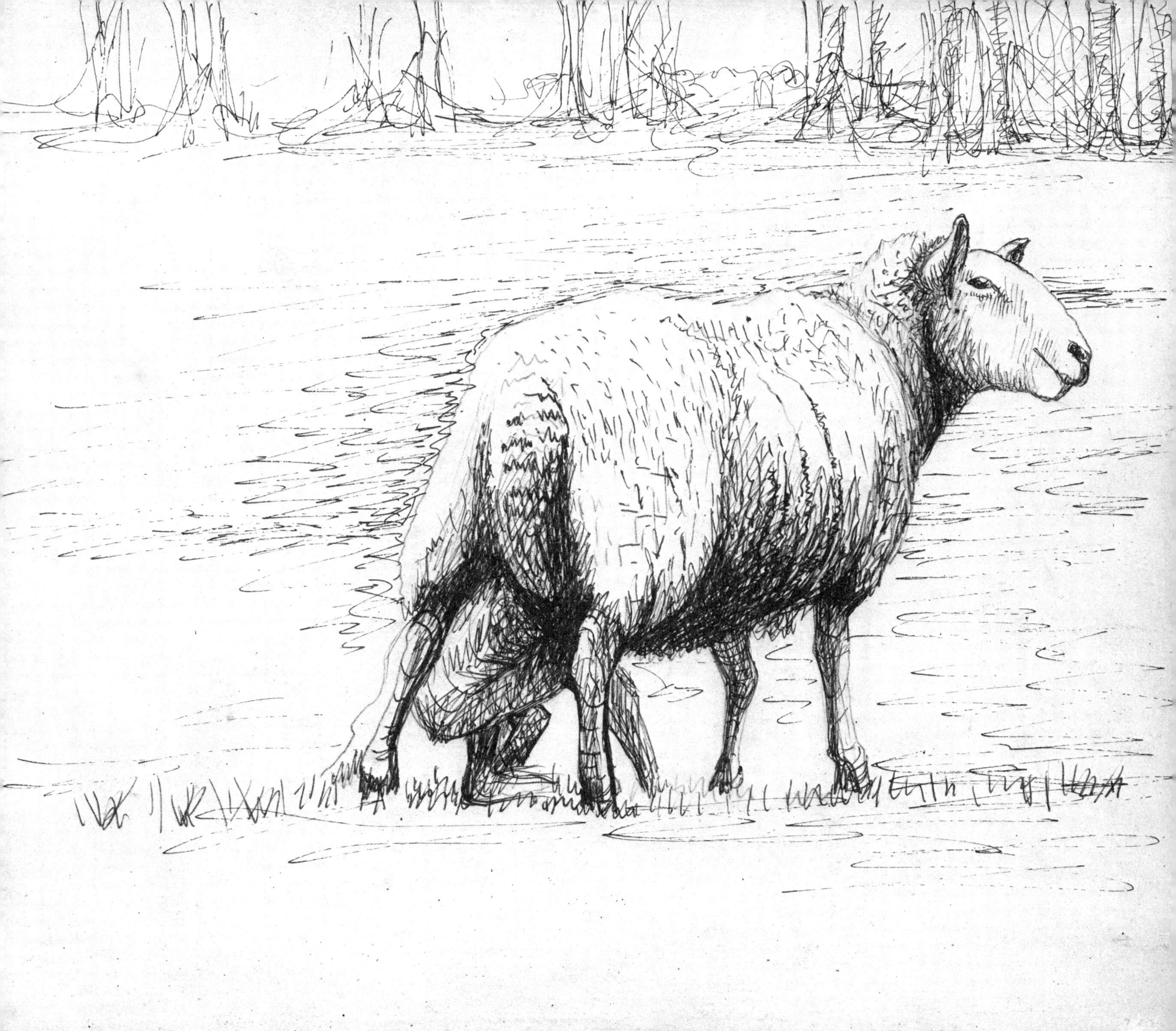

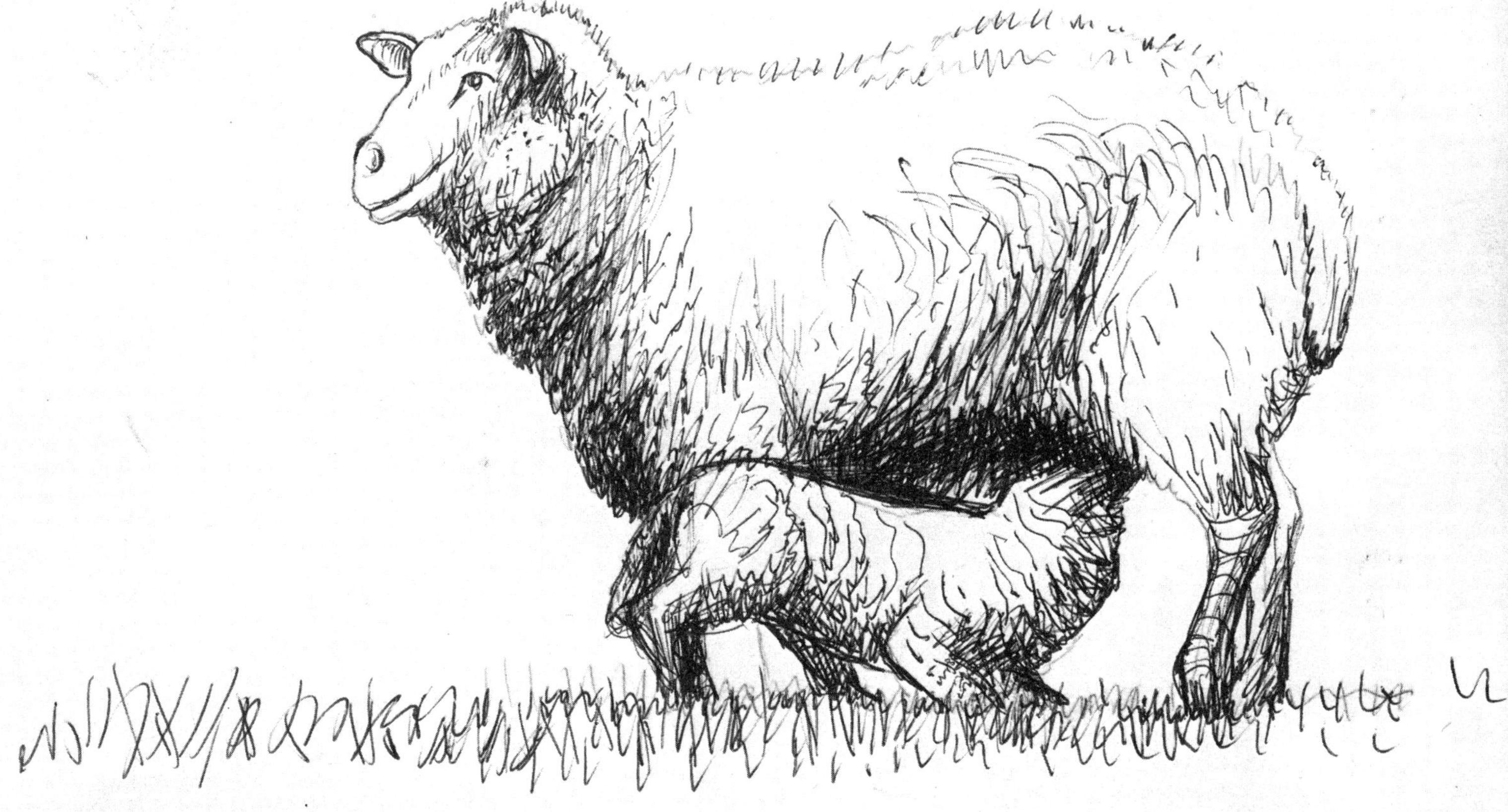

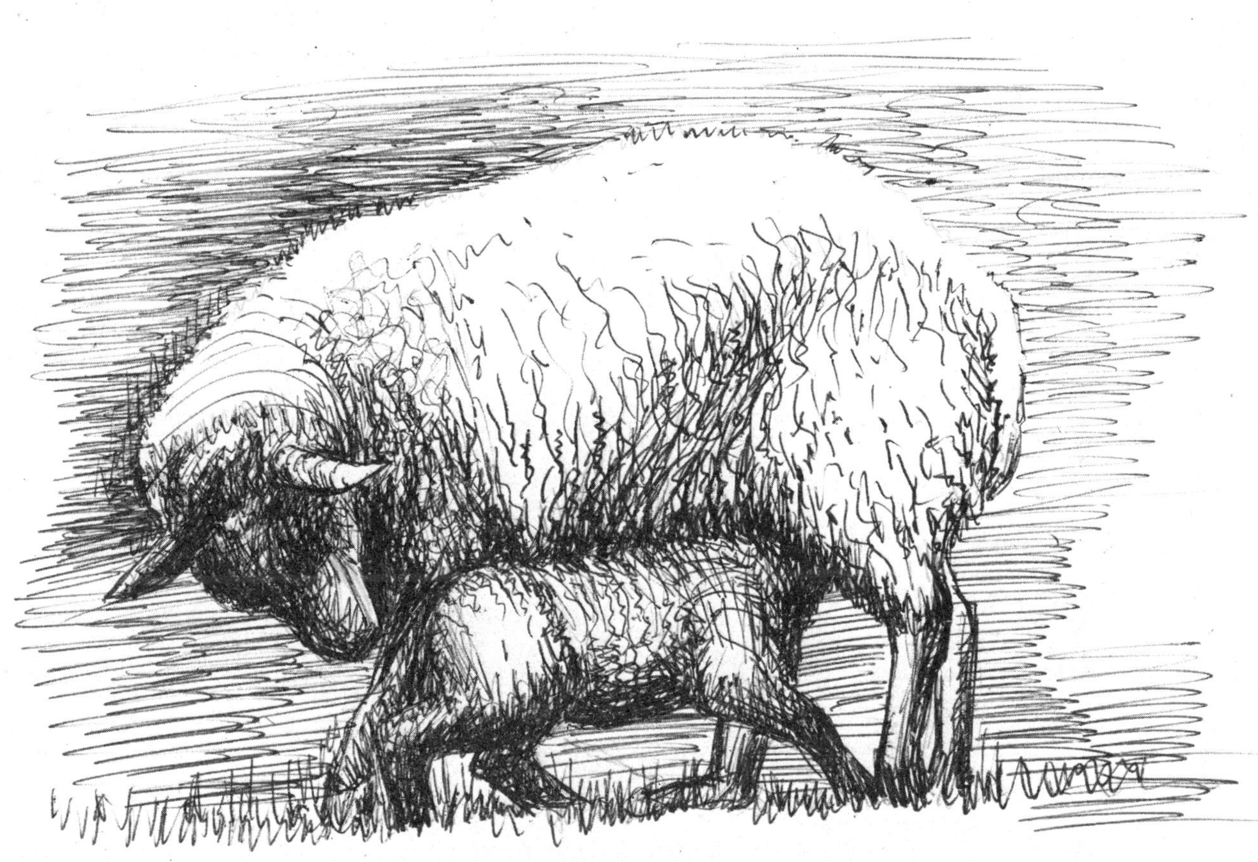

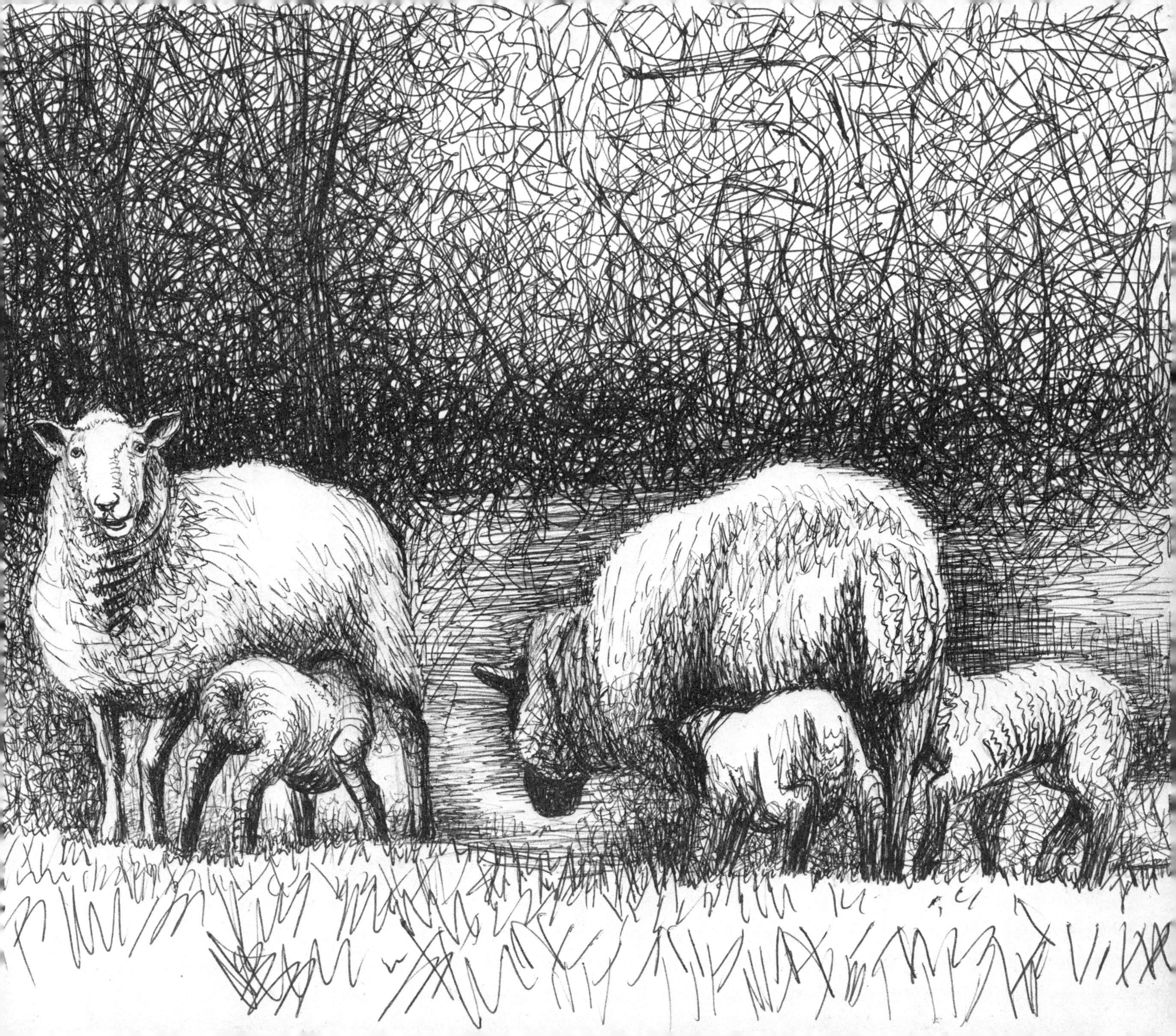

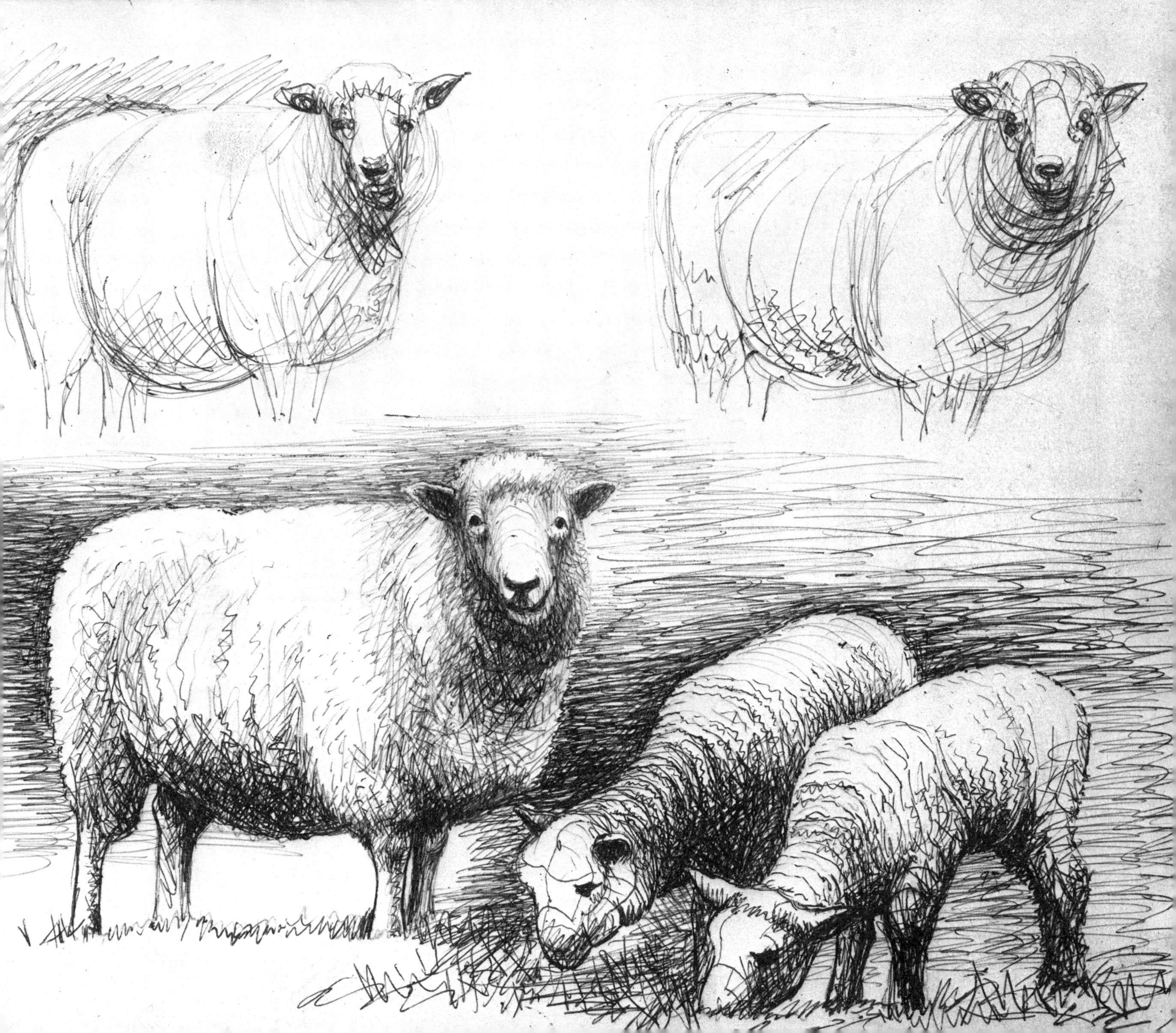

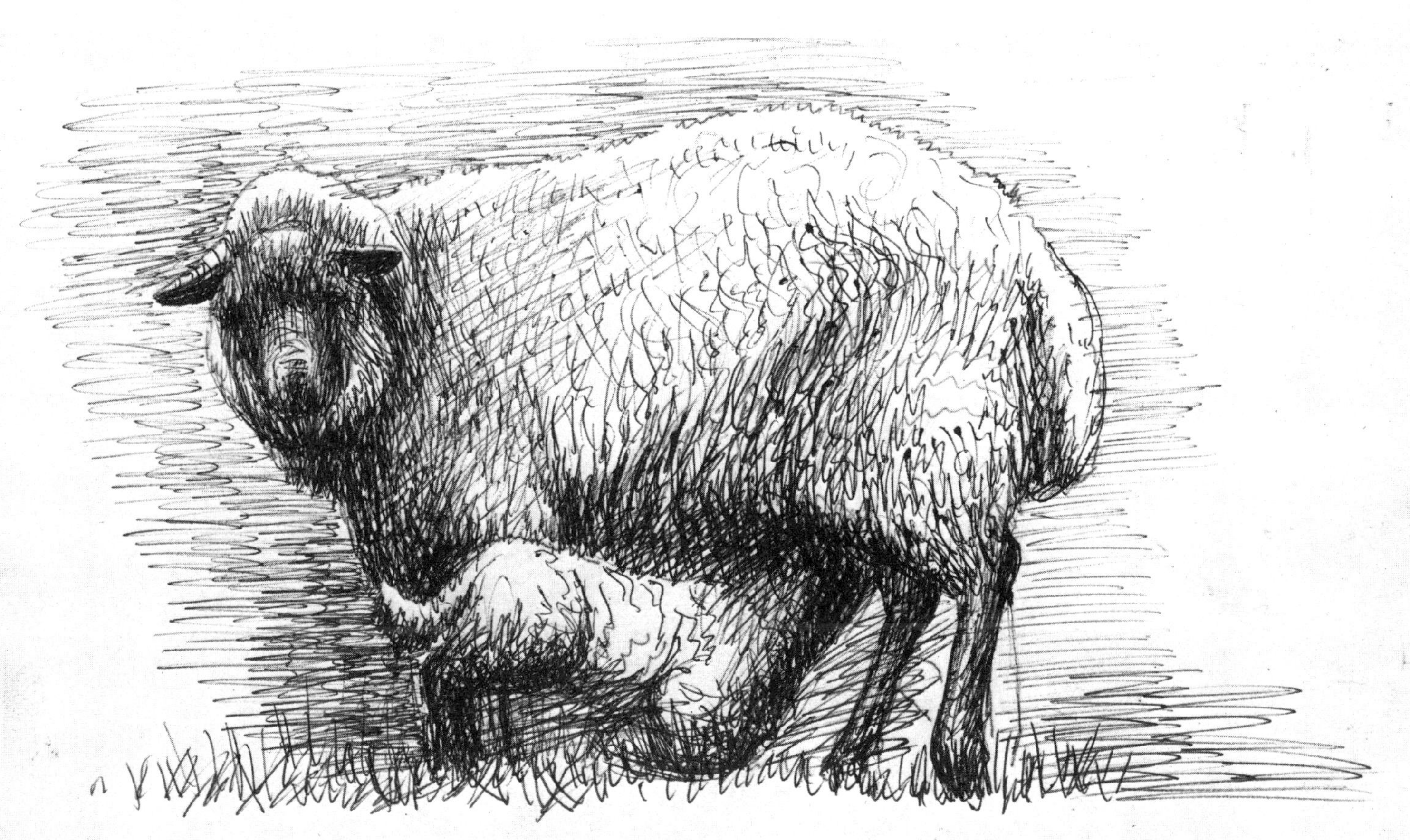

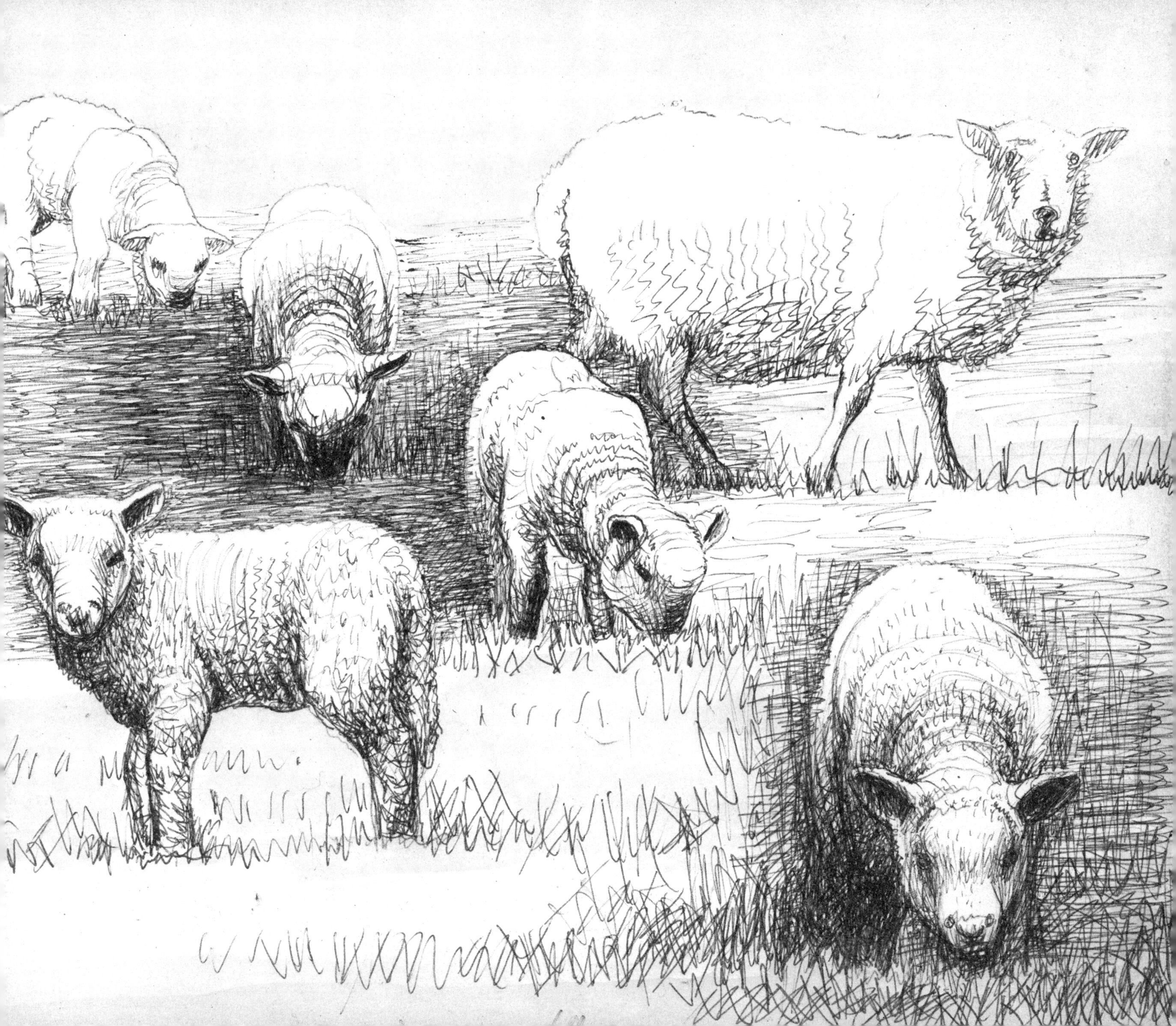

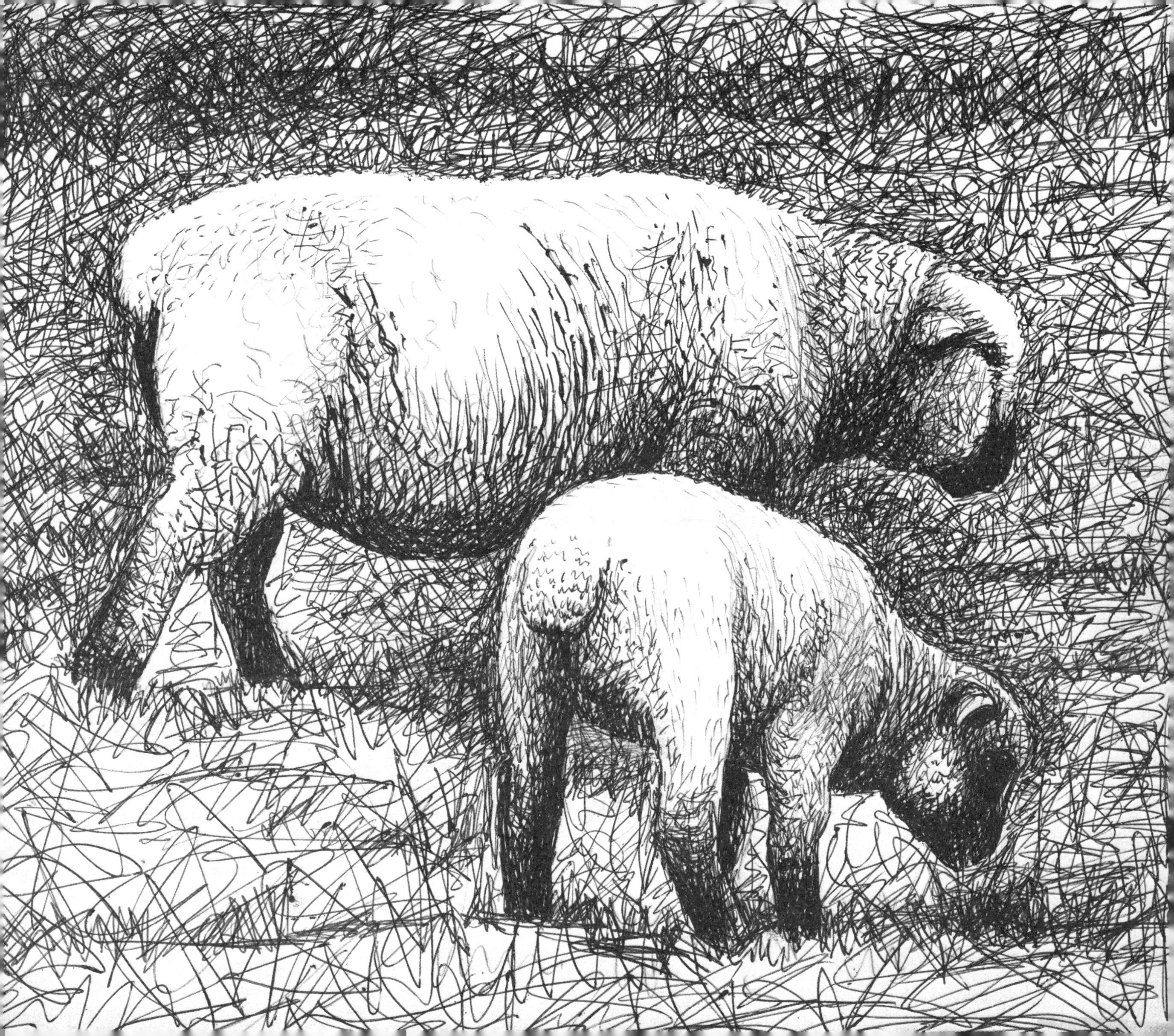

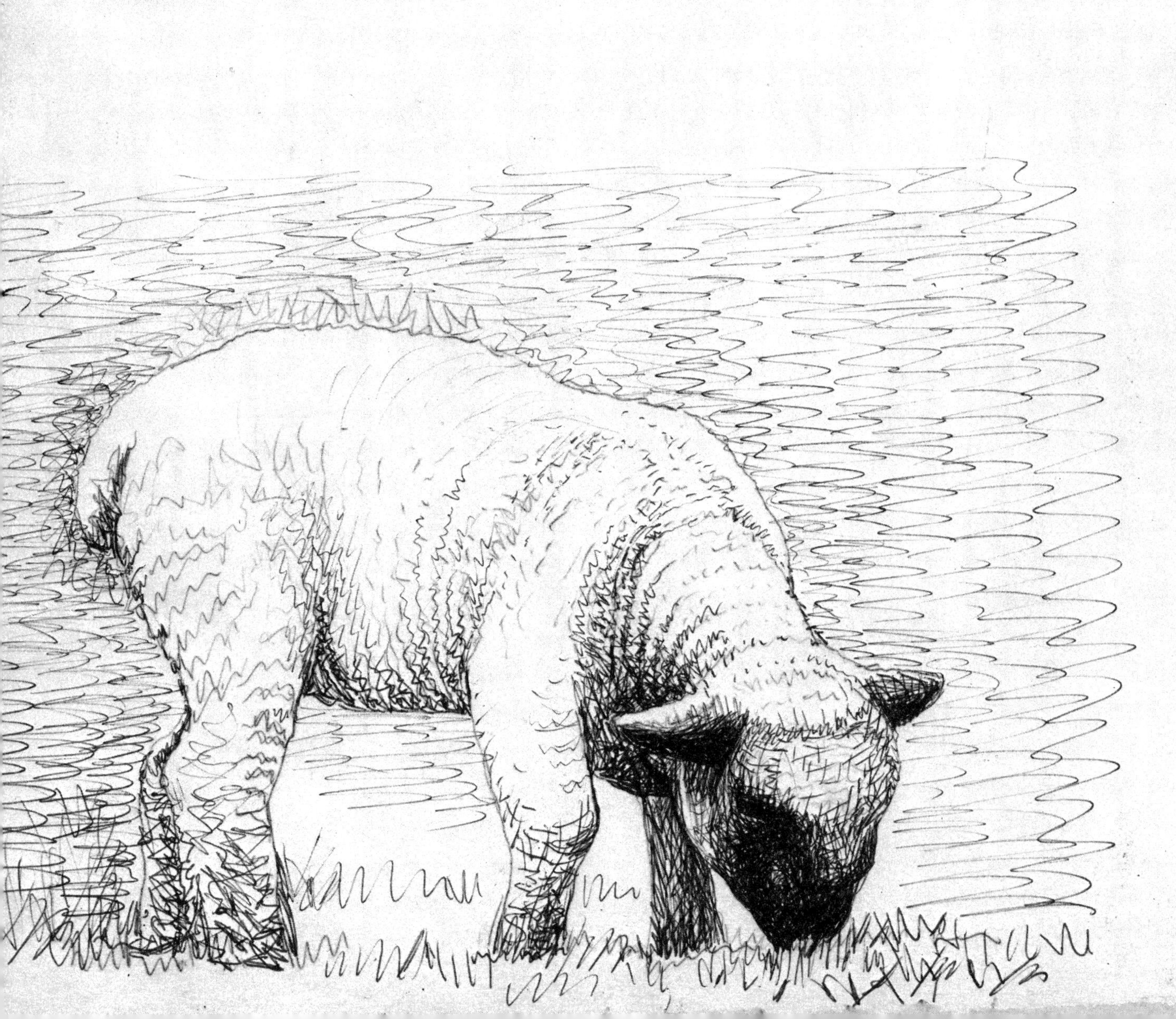

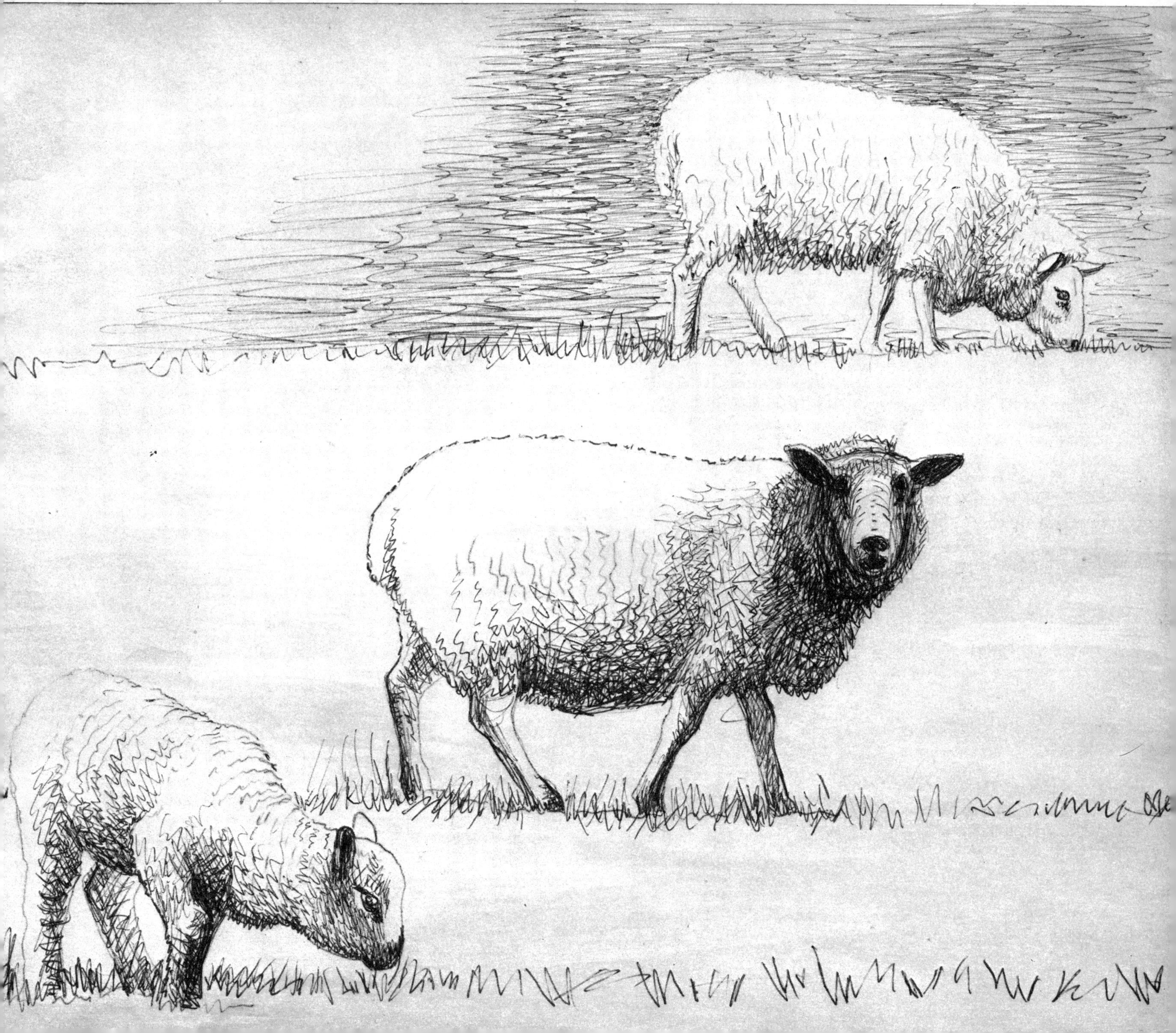

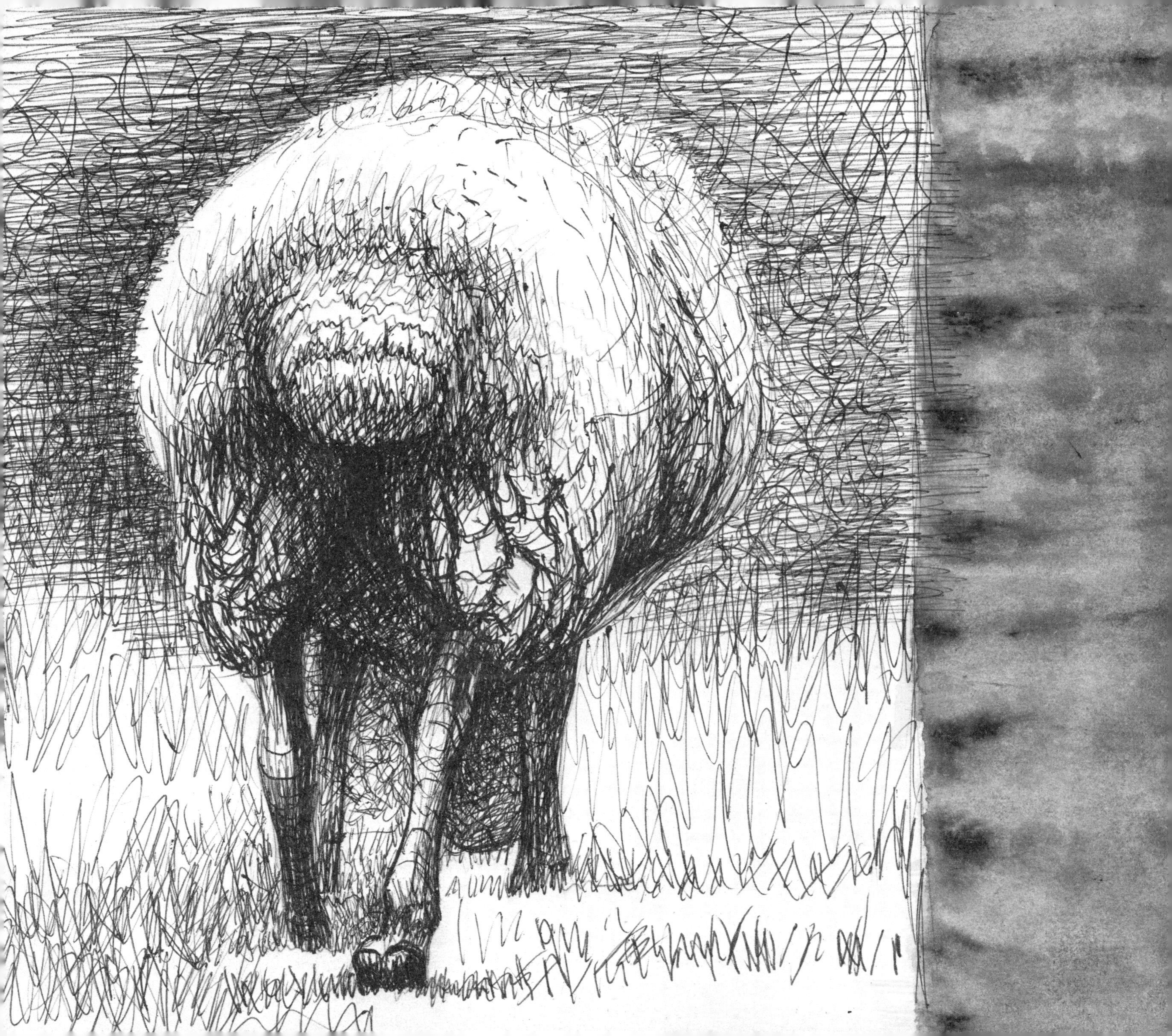

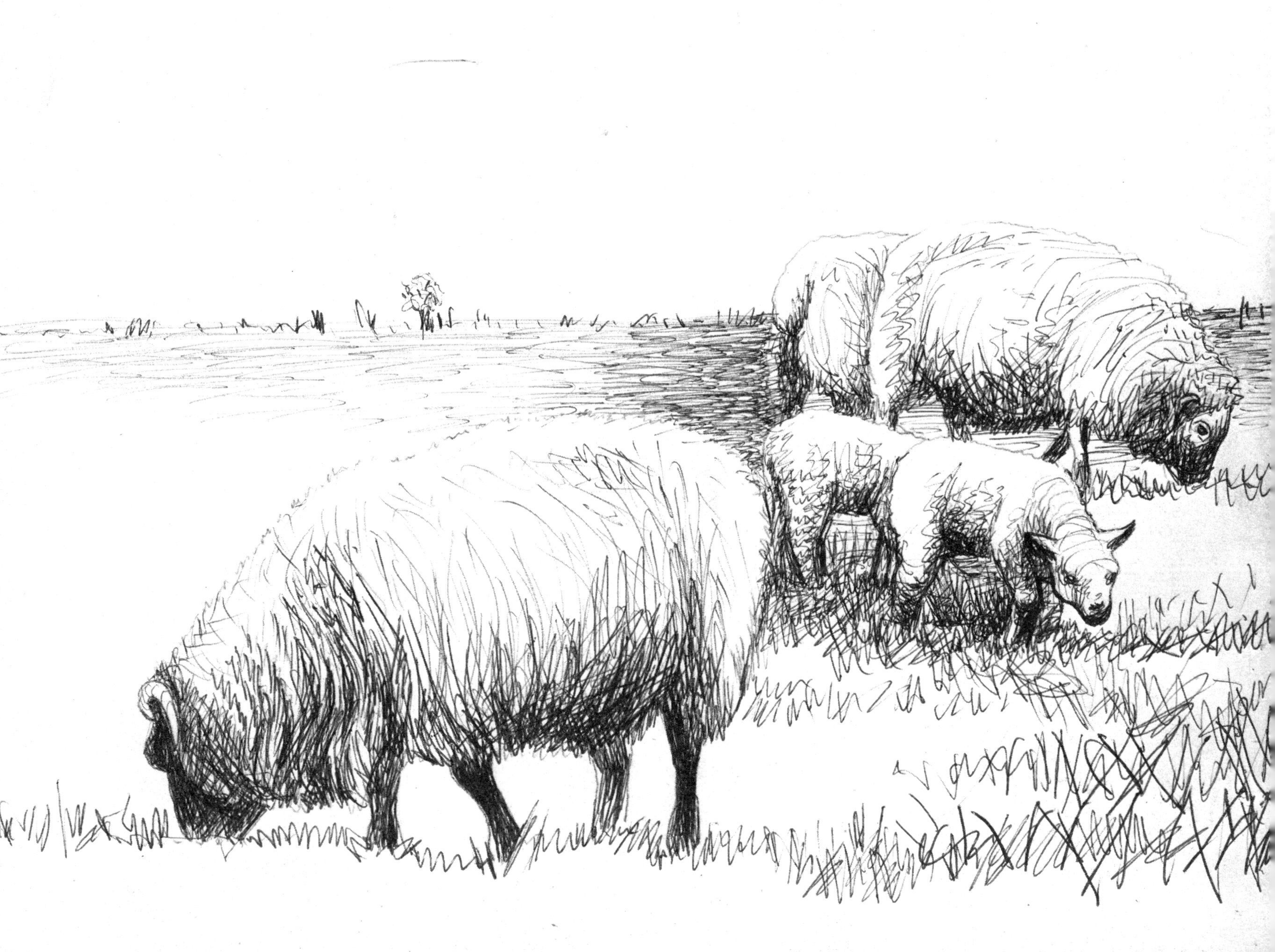

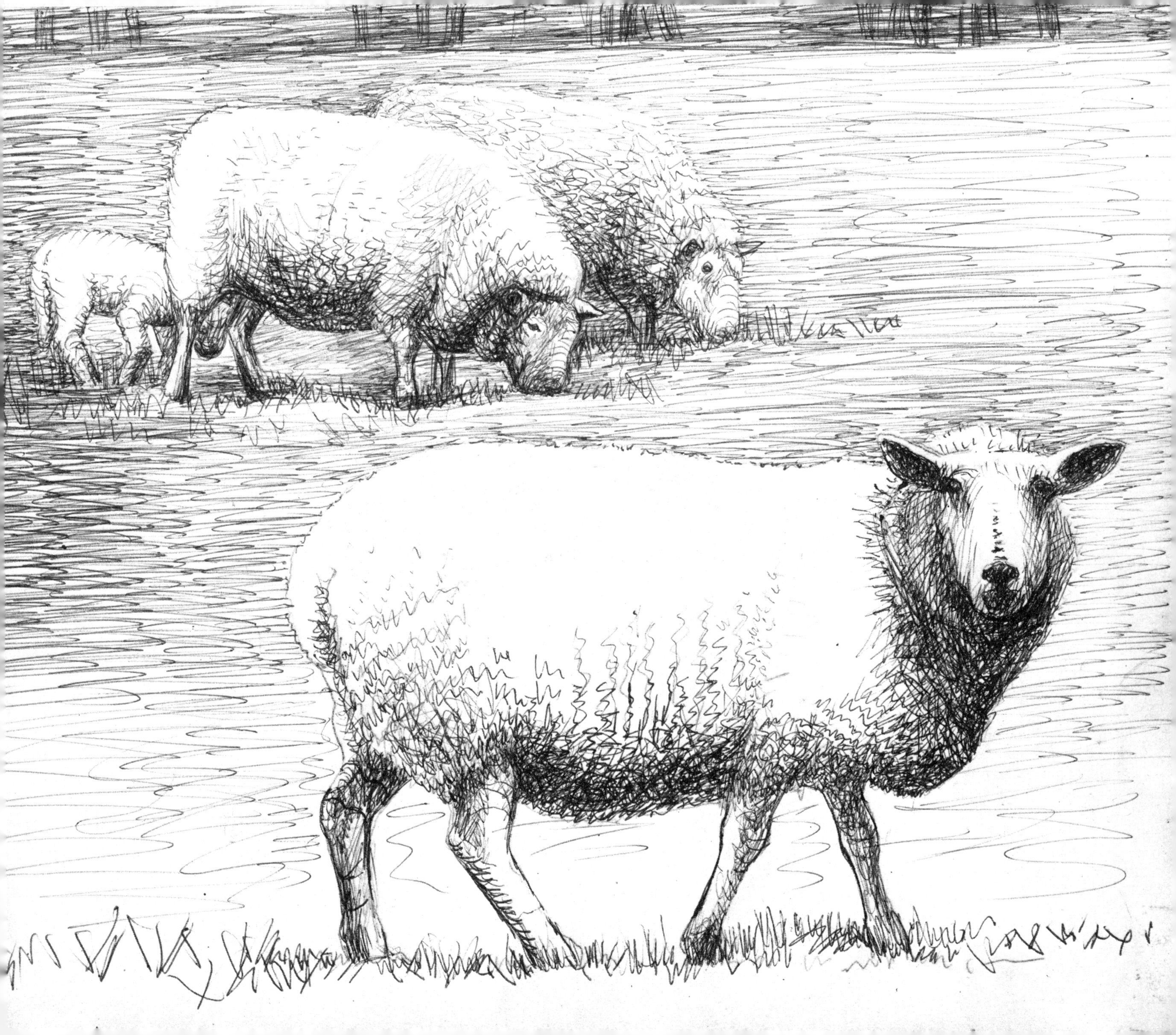

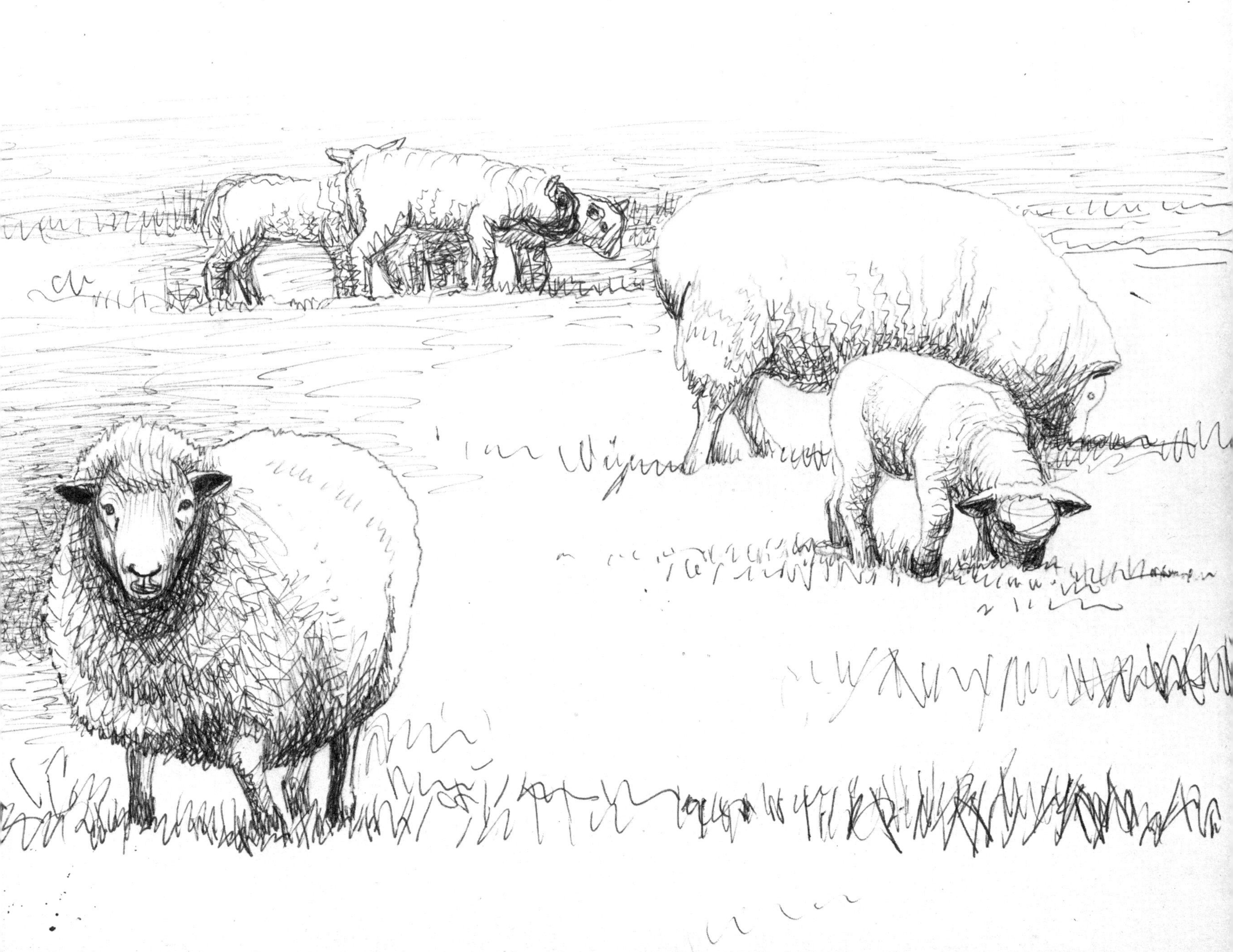

14

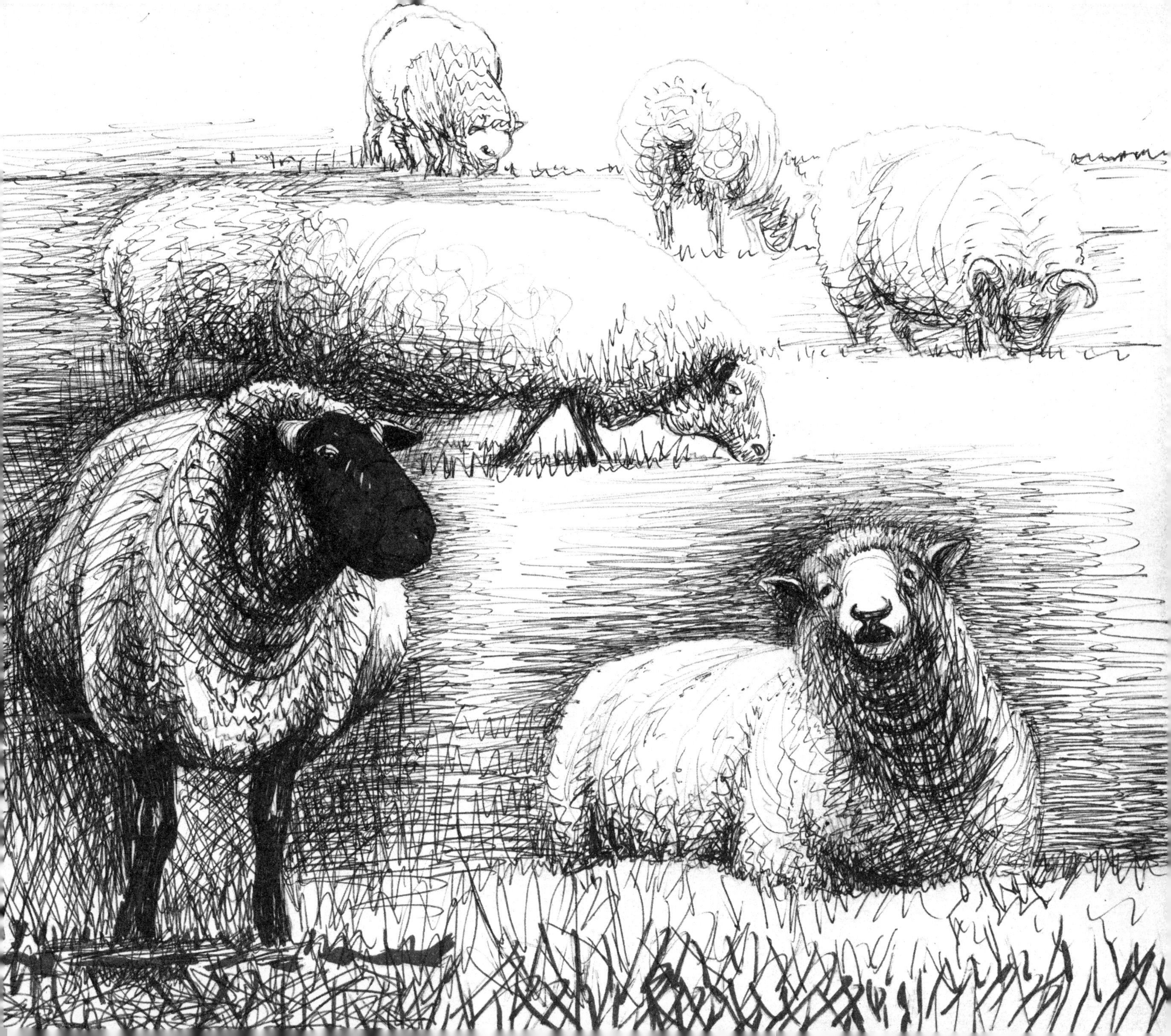

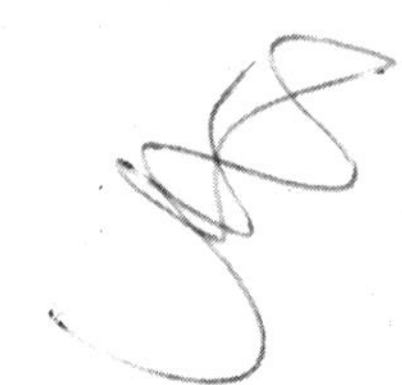
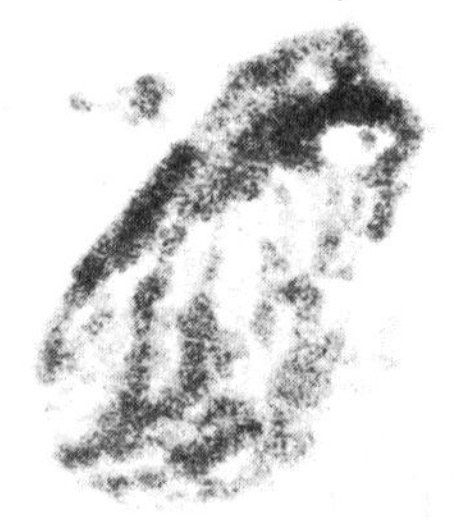

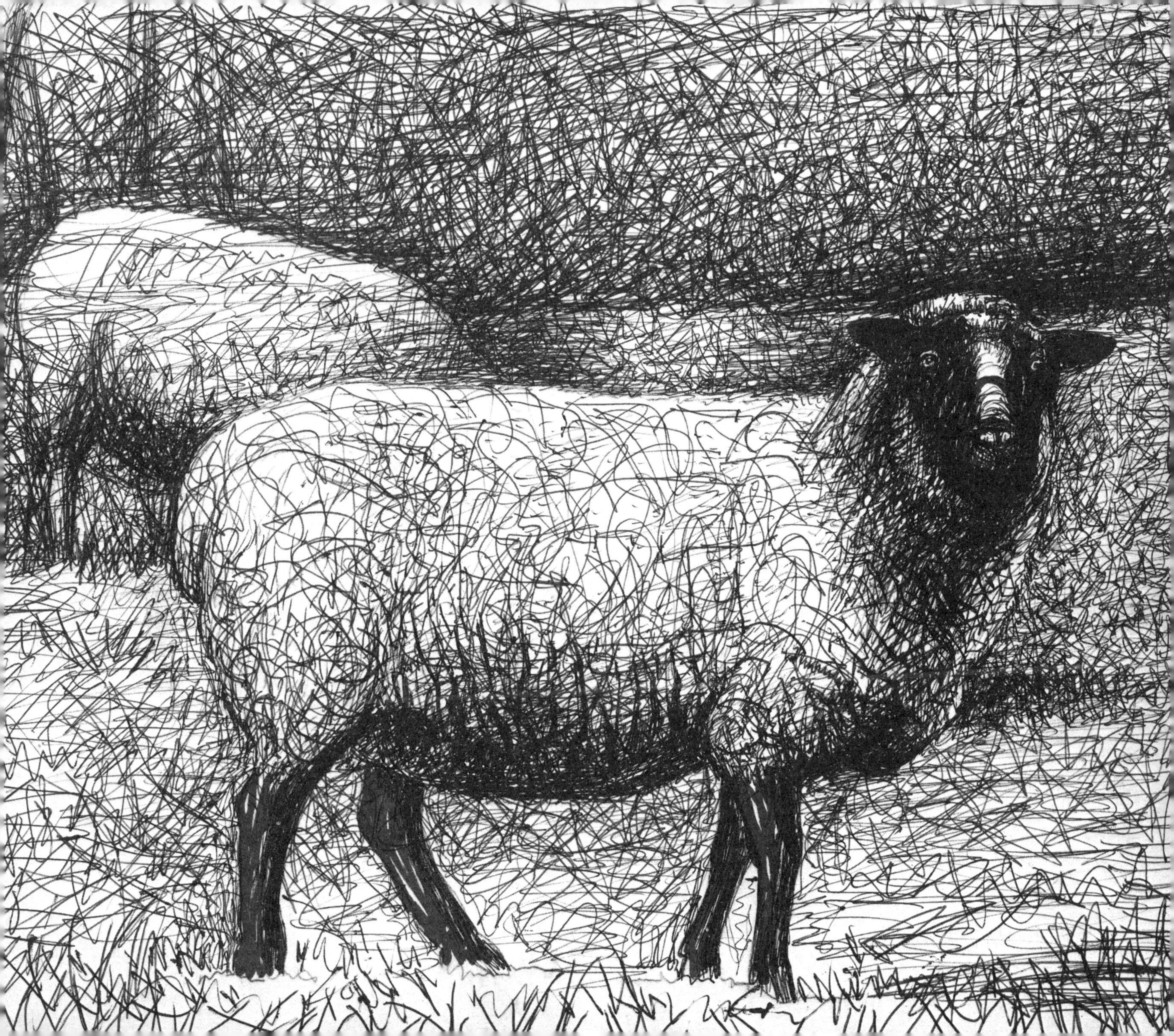

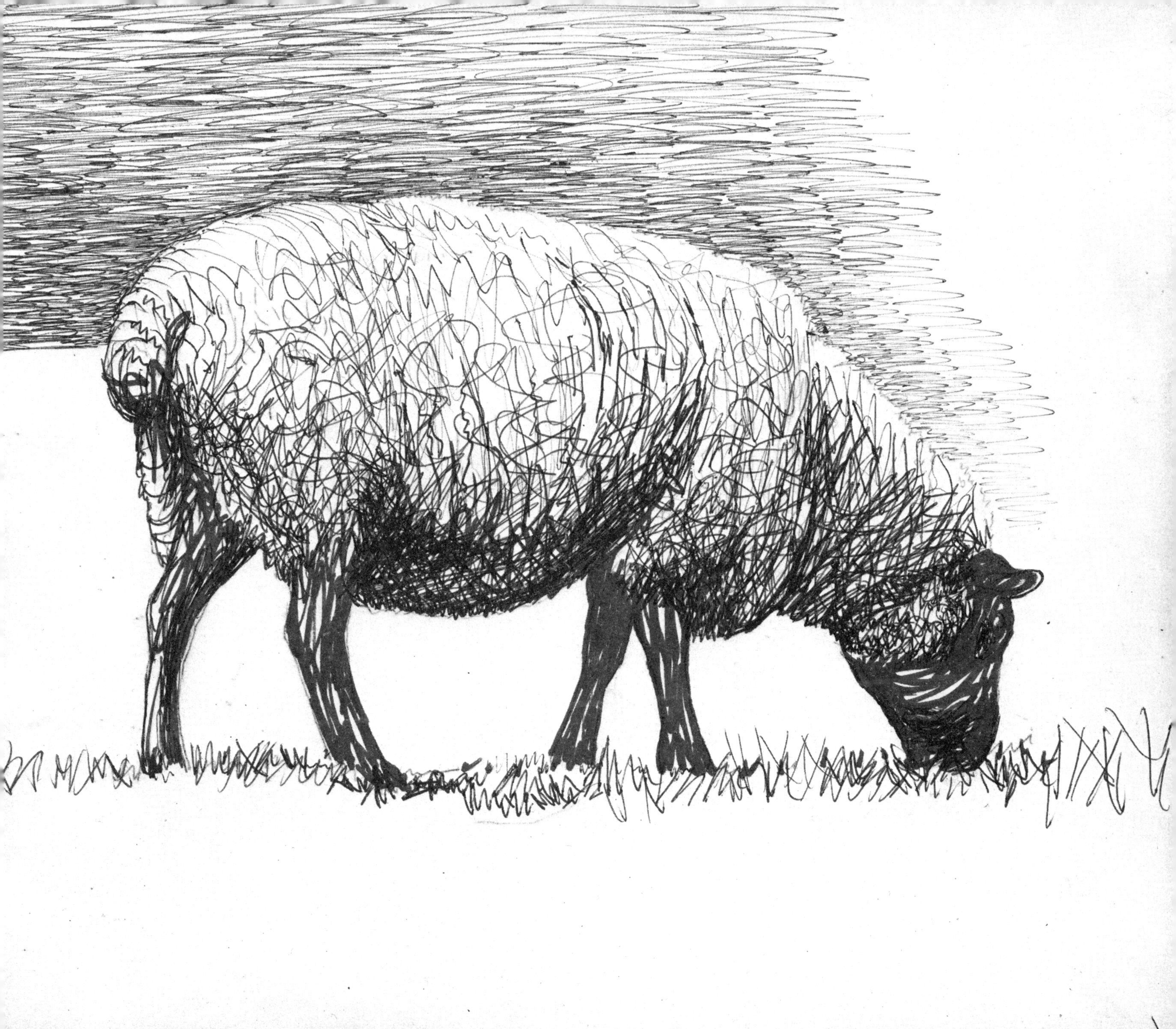

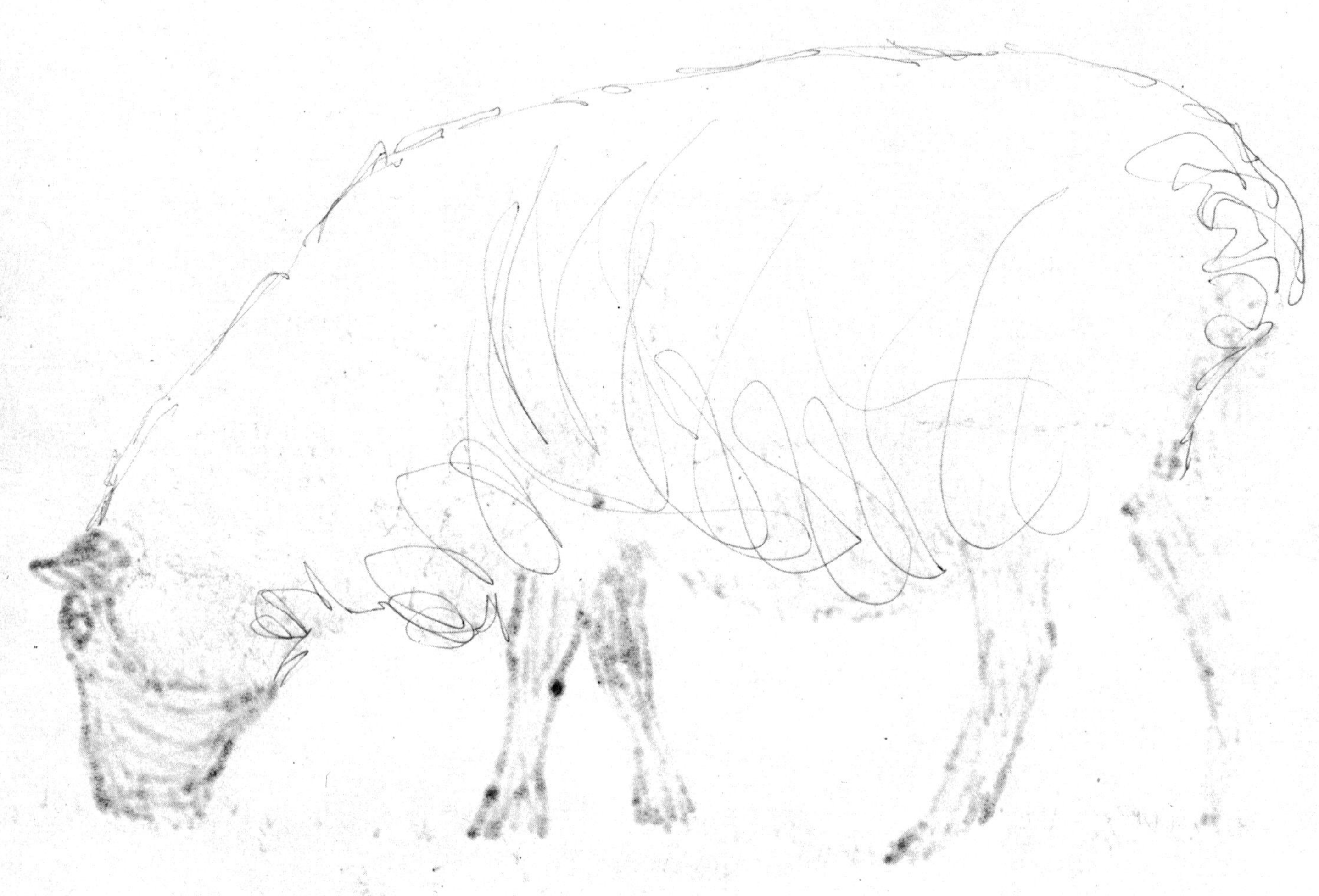

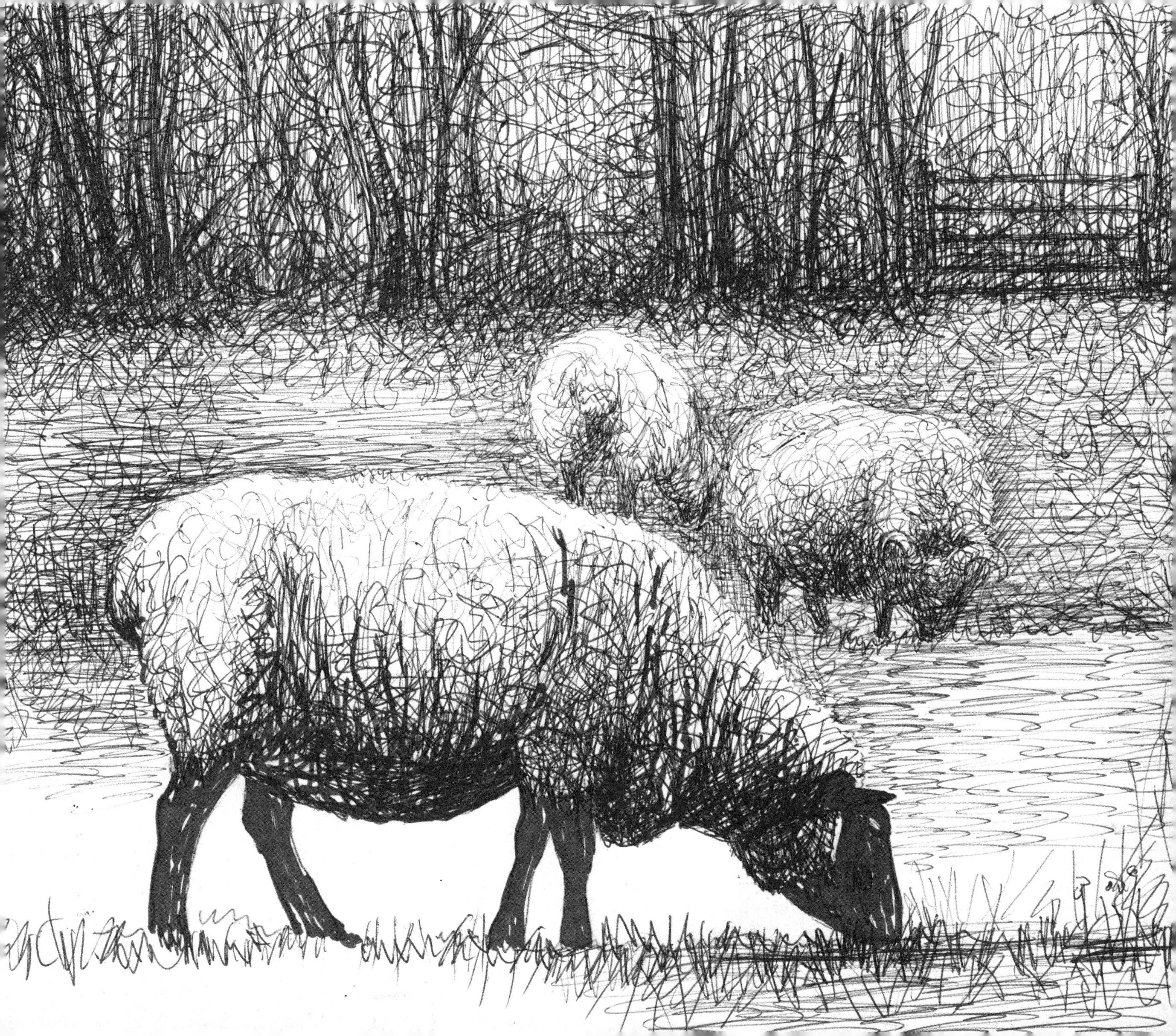

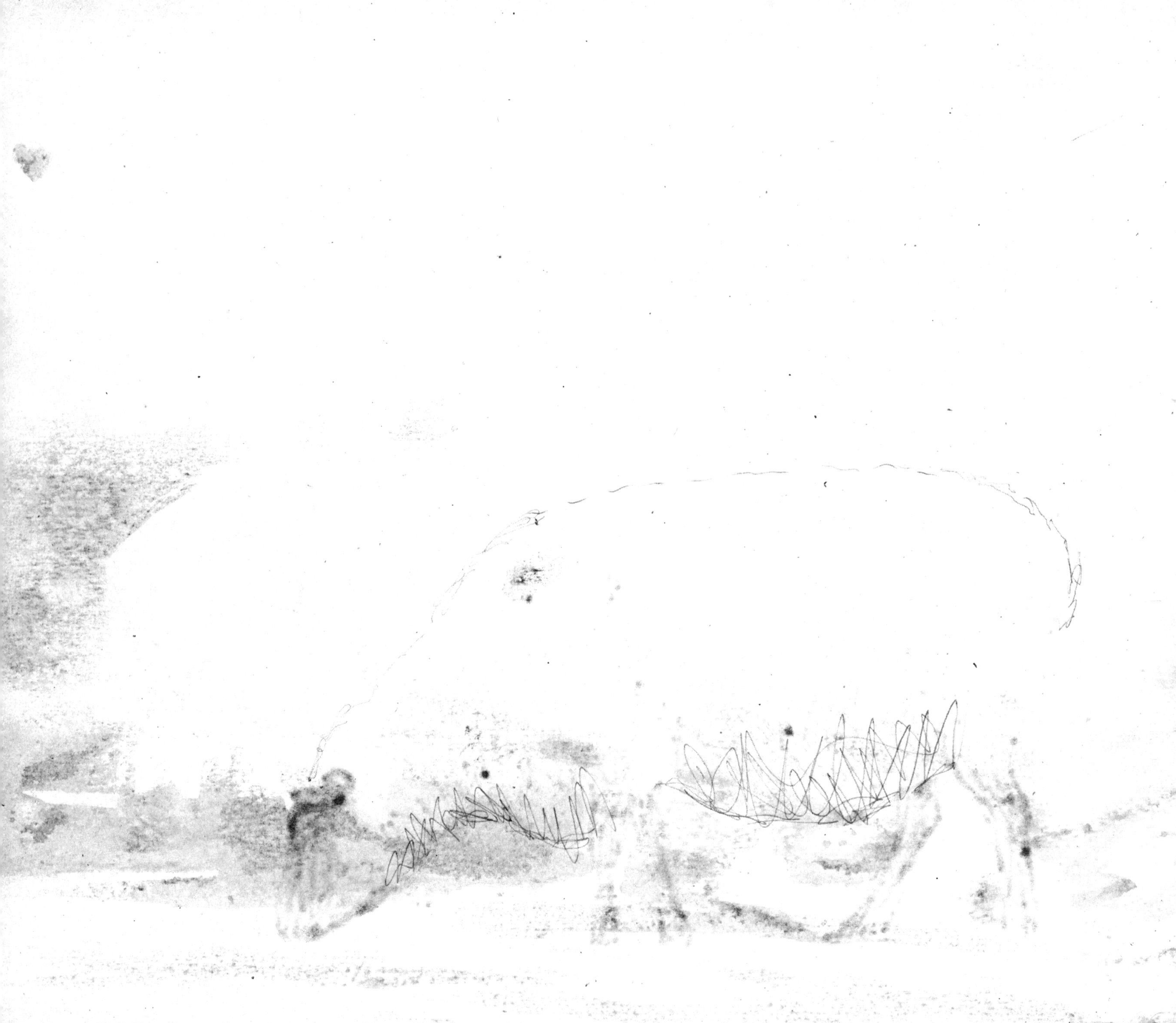

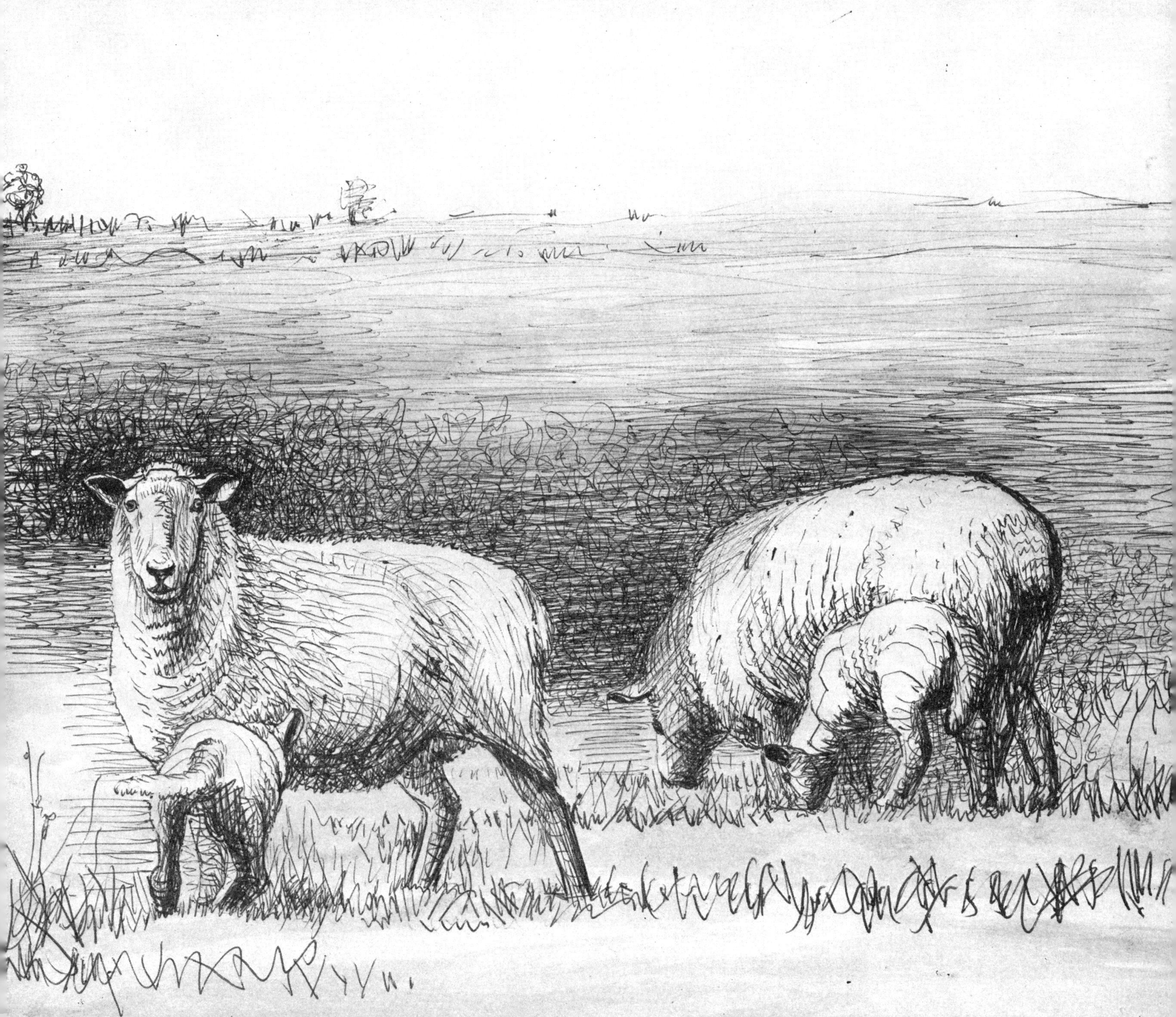

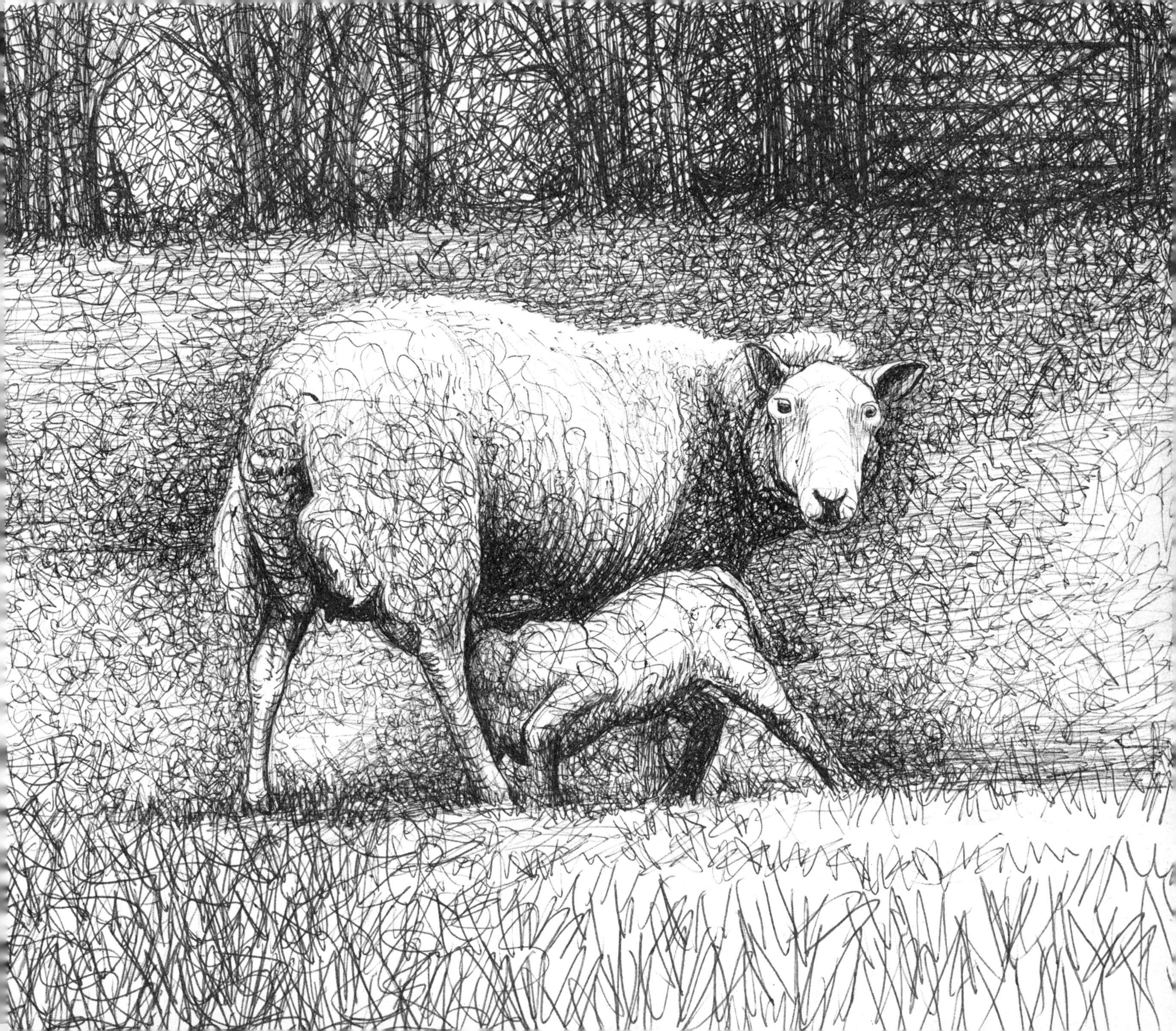

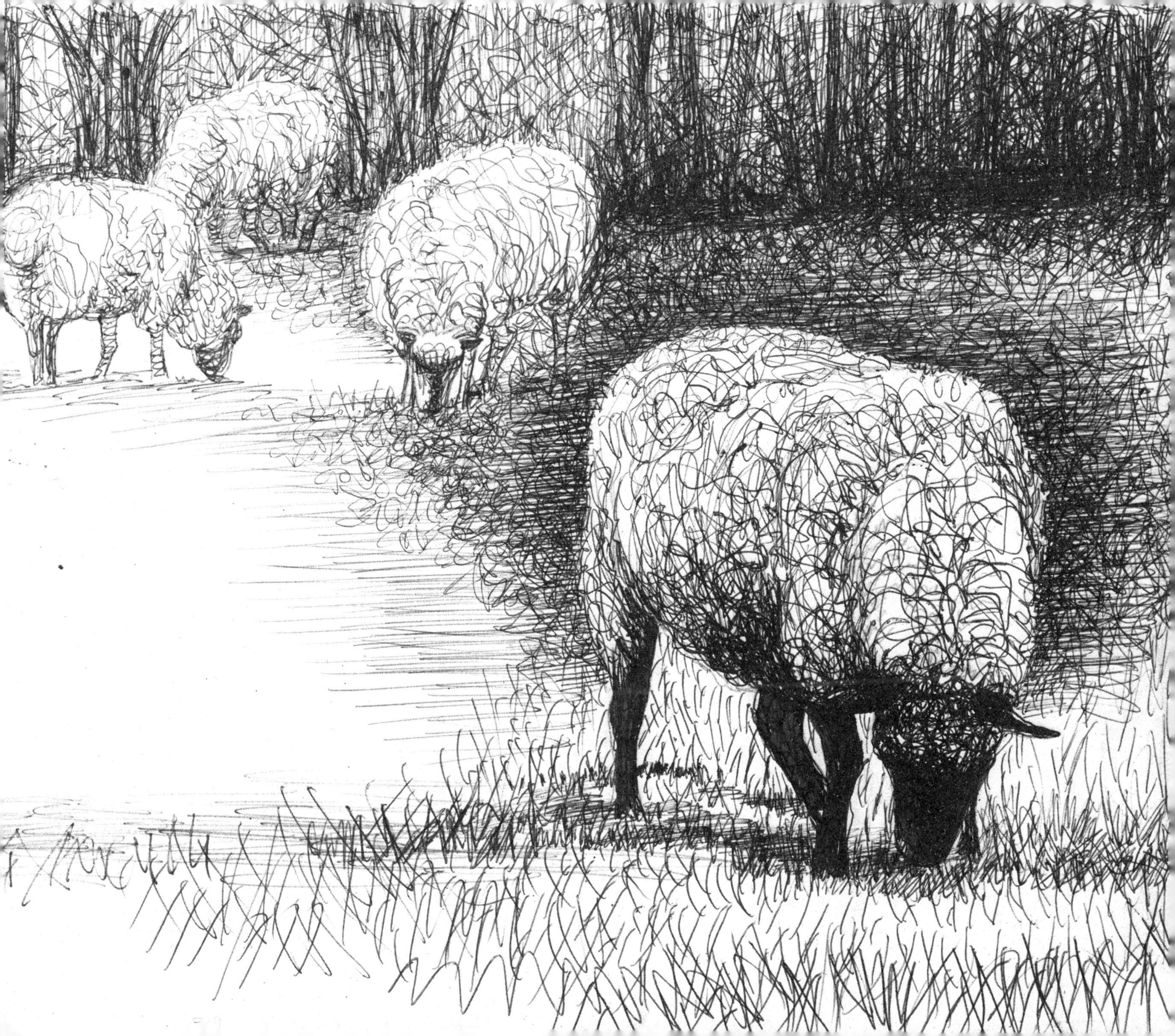

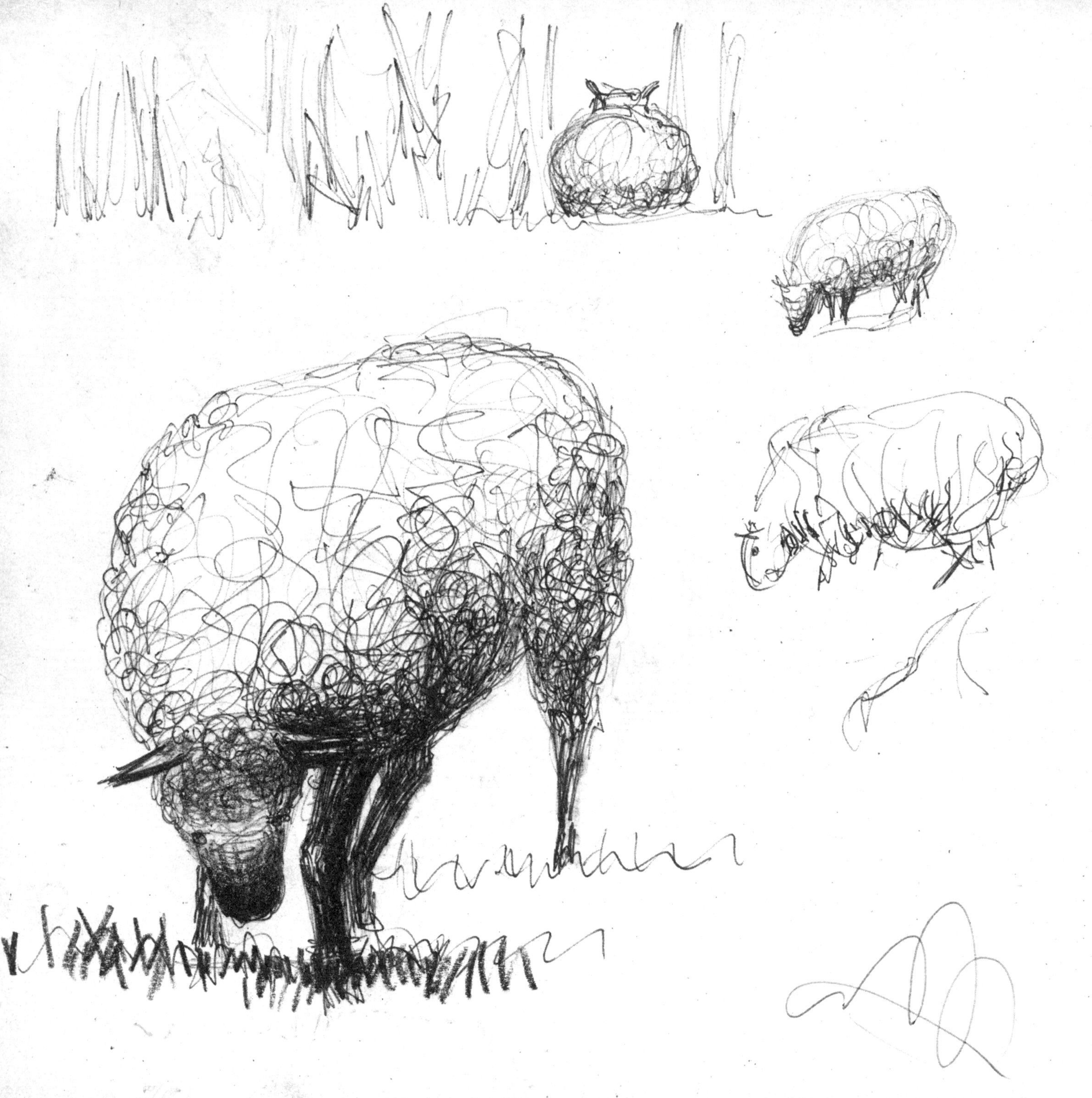

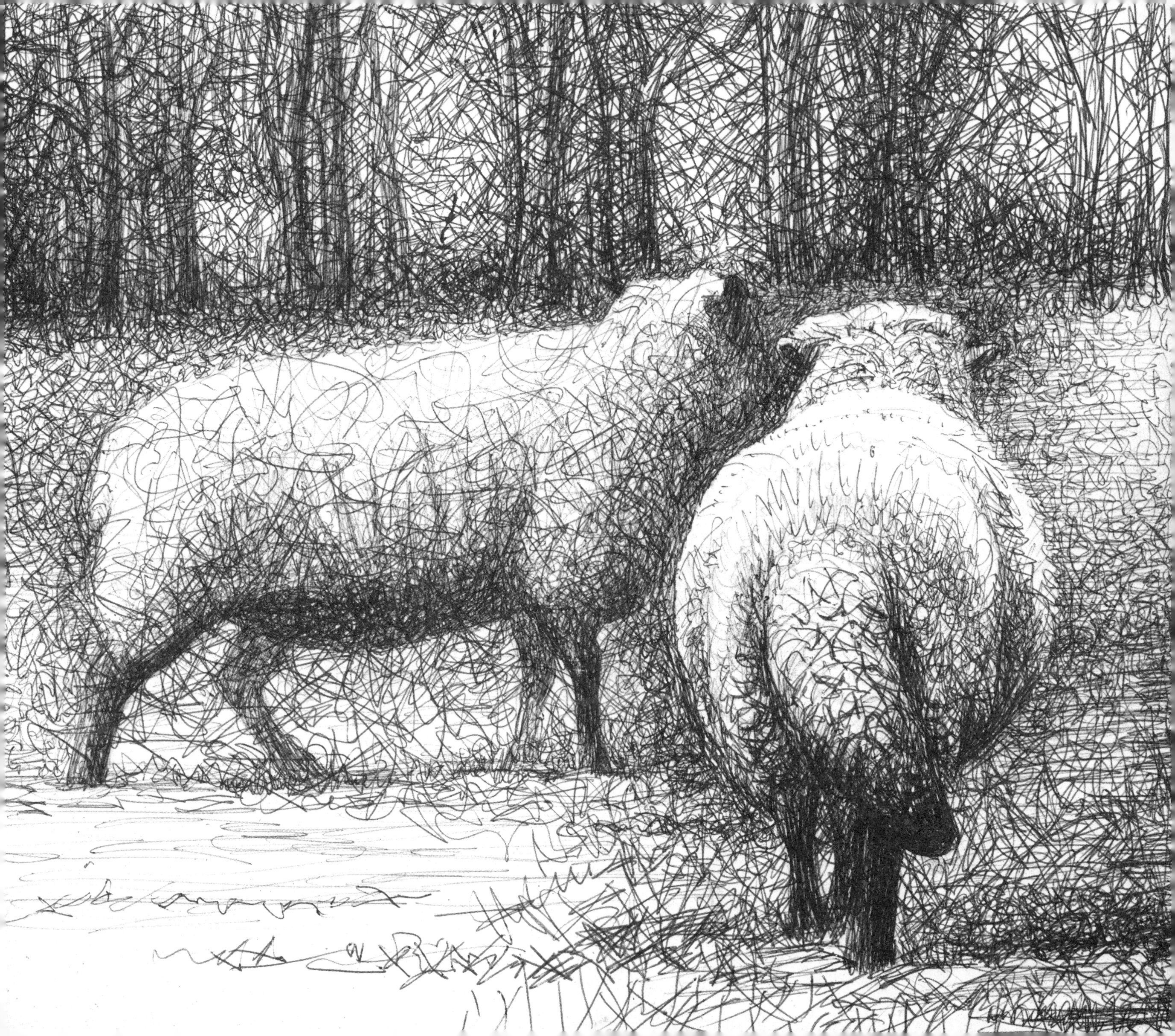

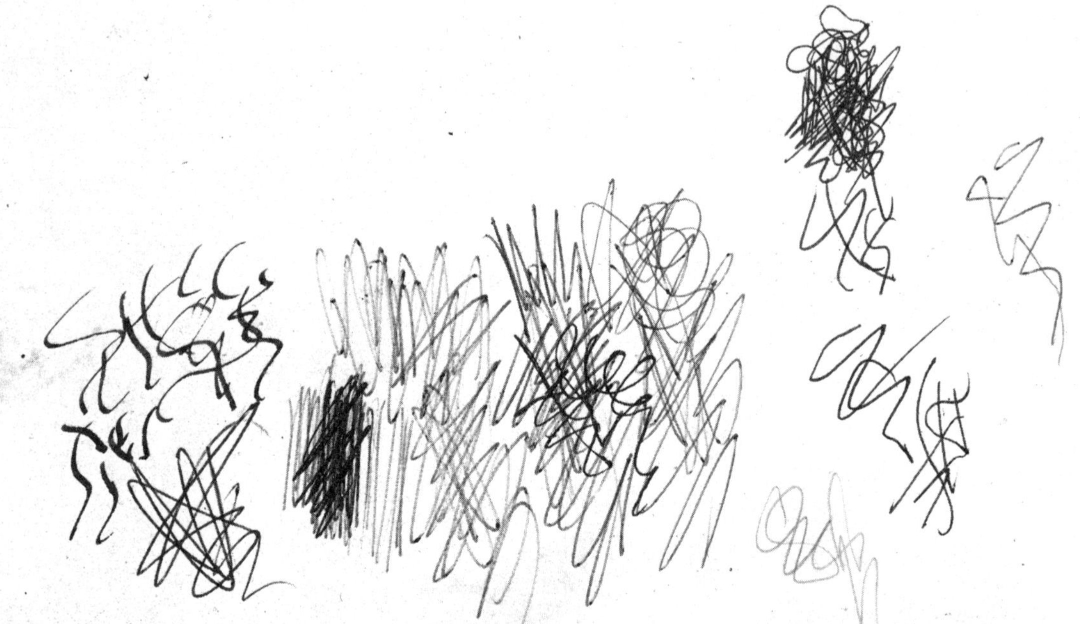

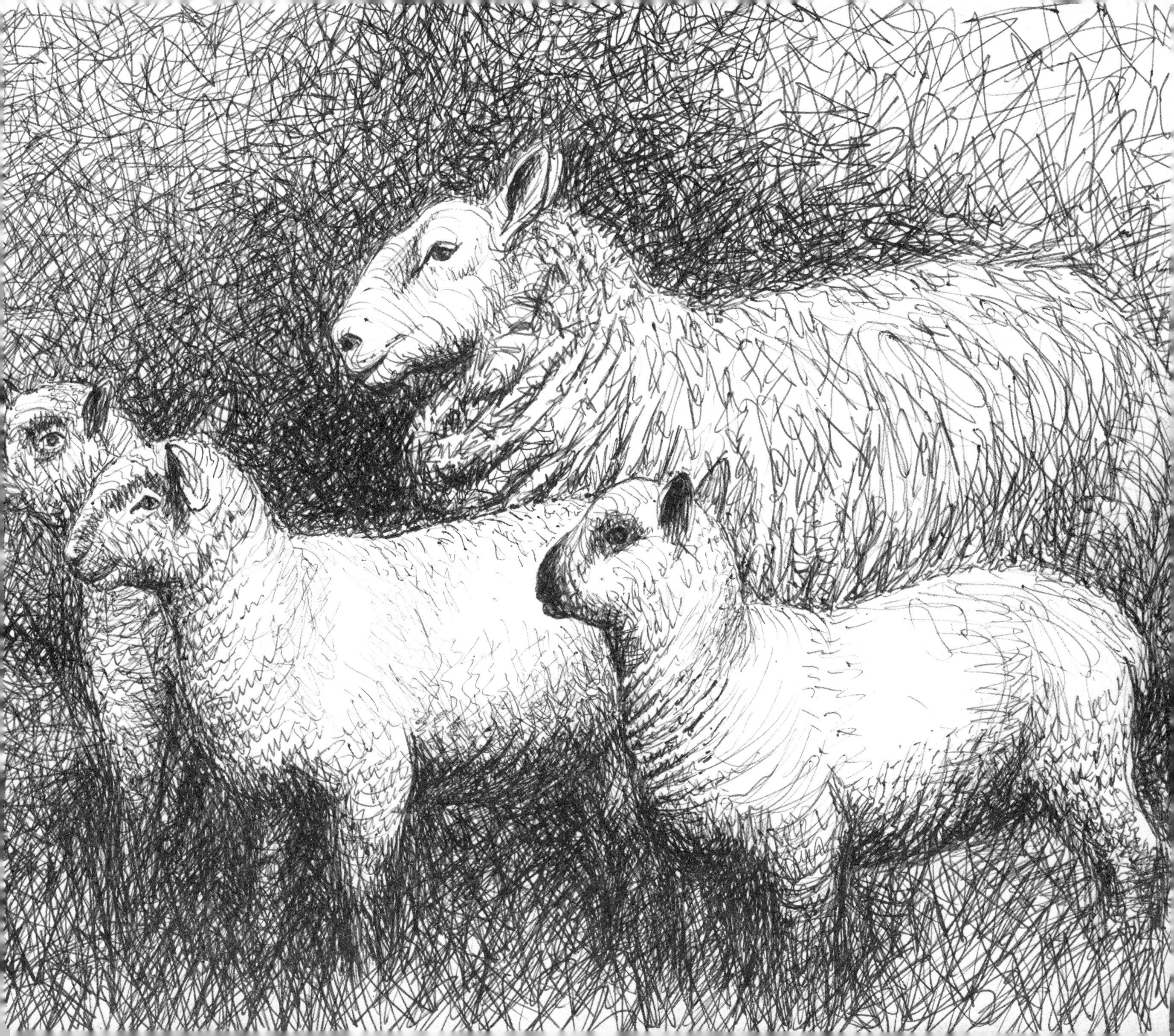

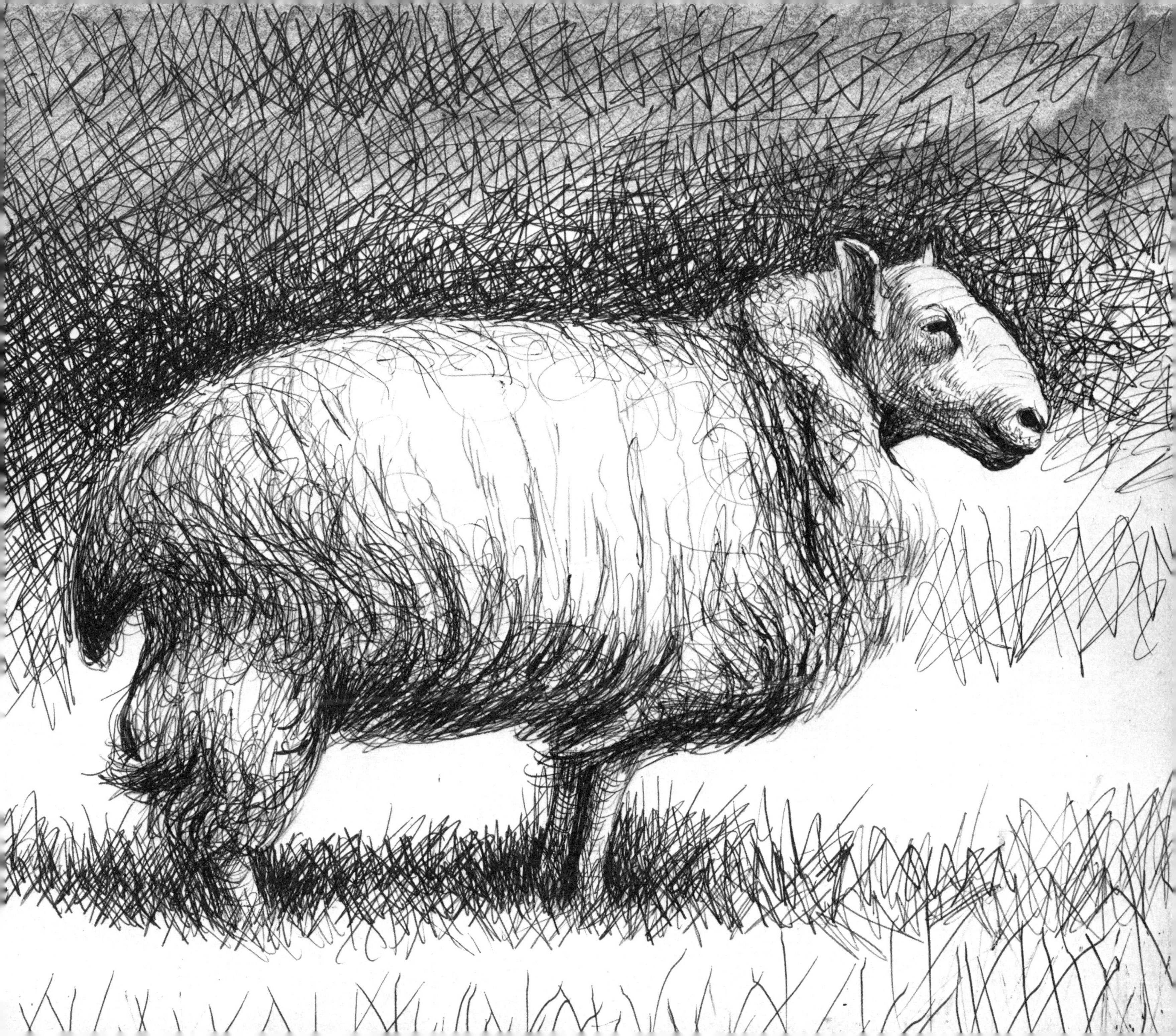

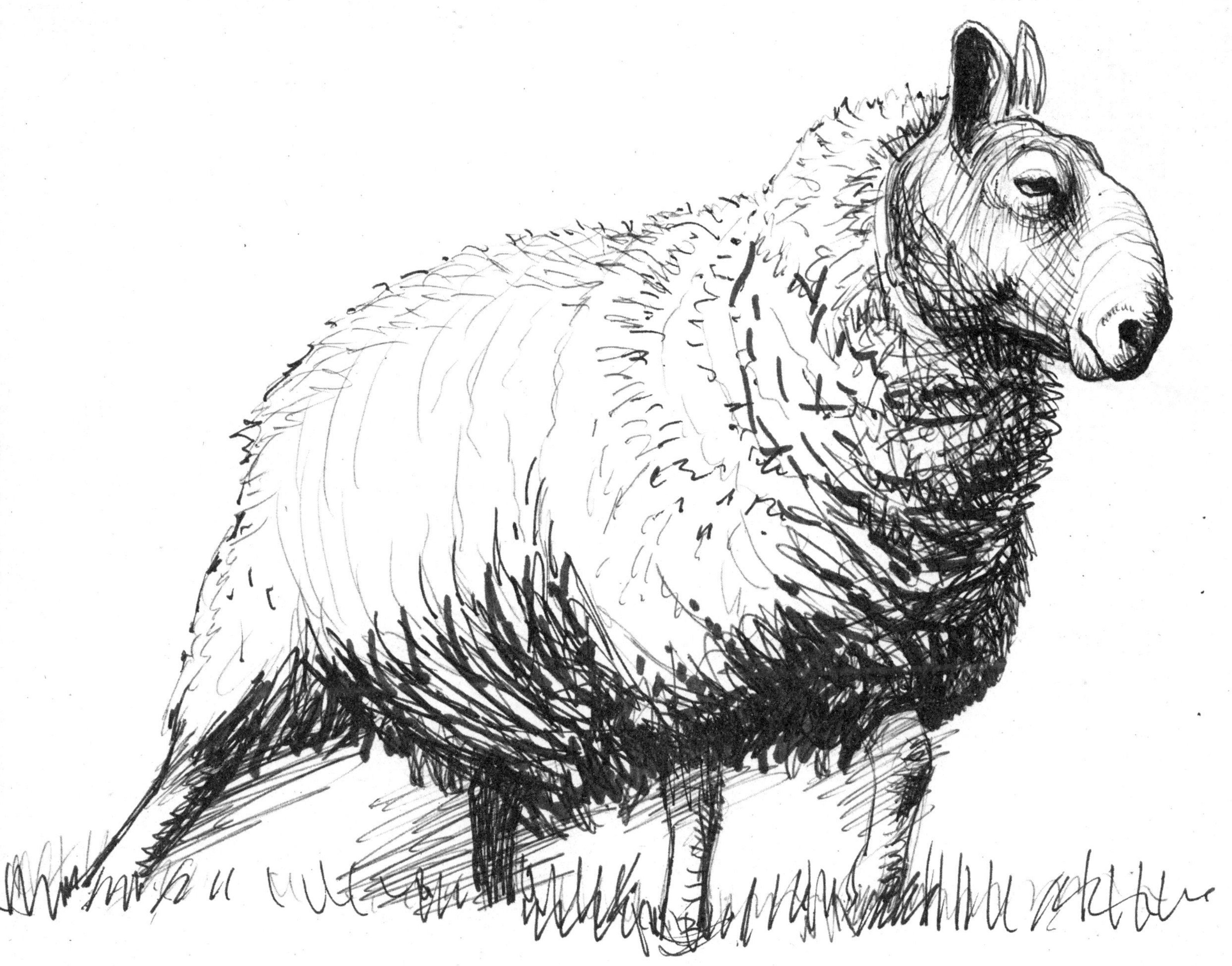

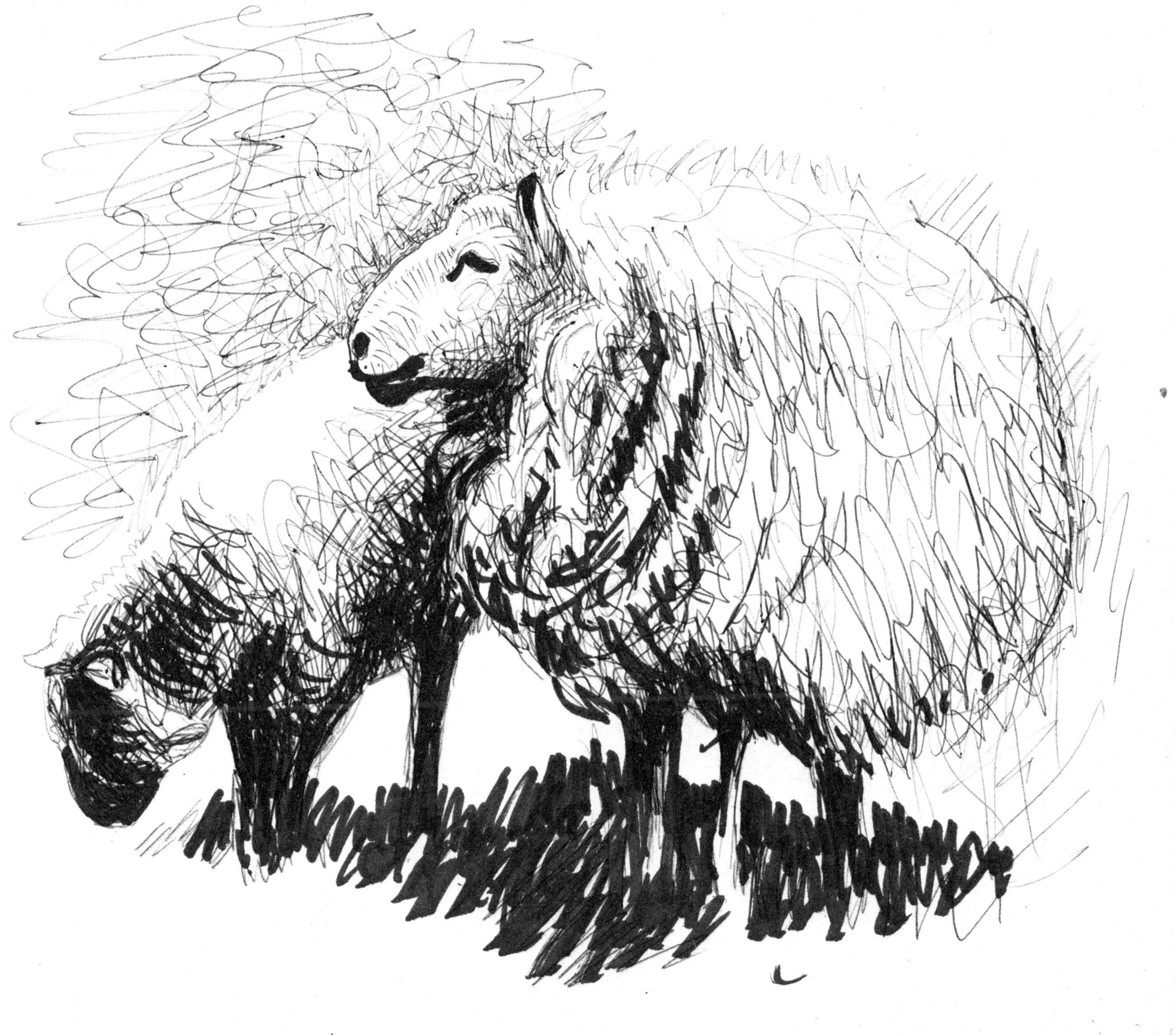

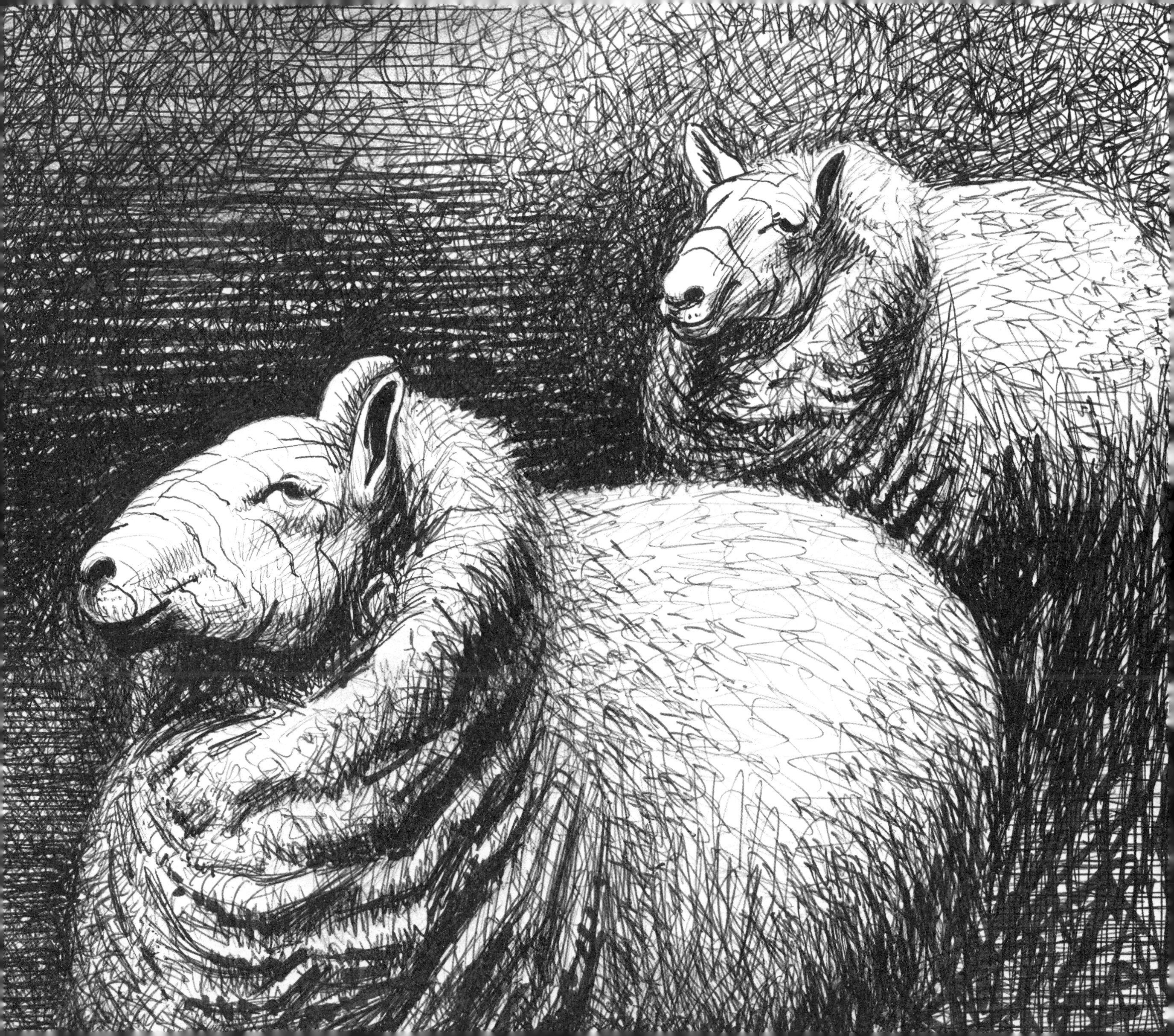

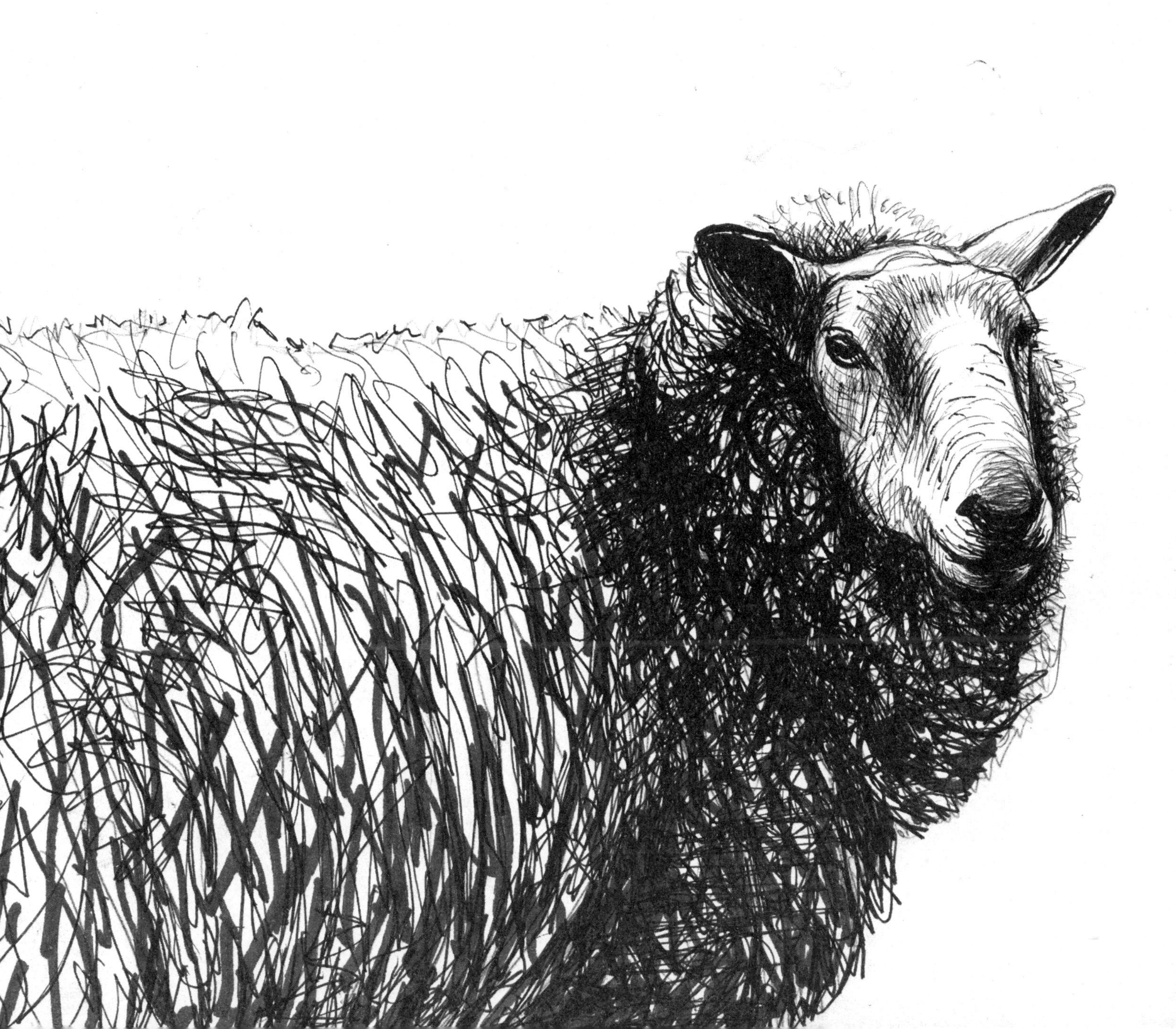

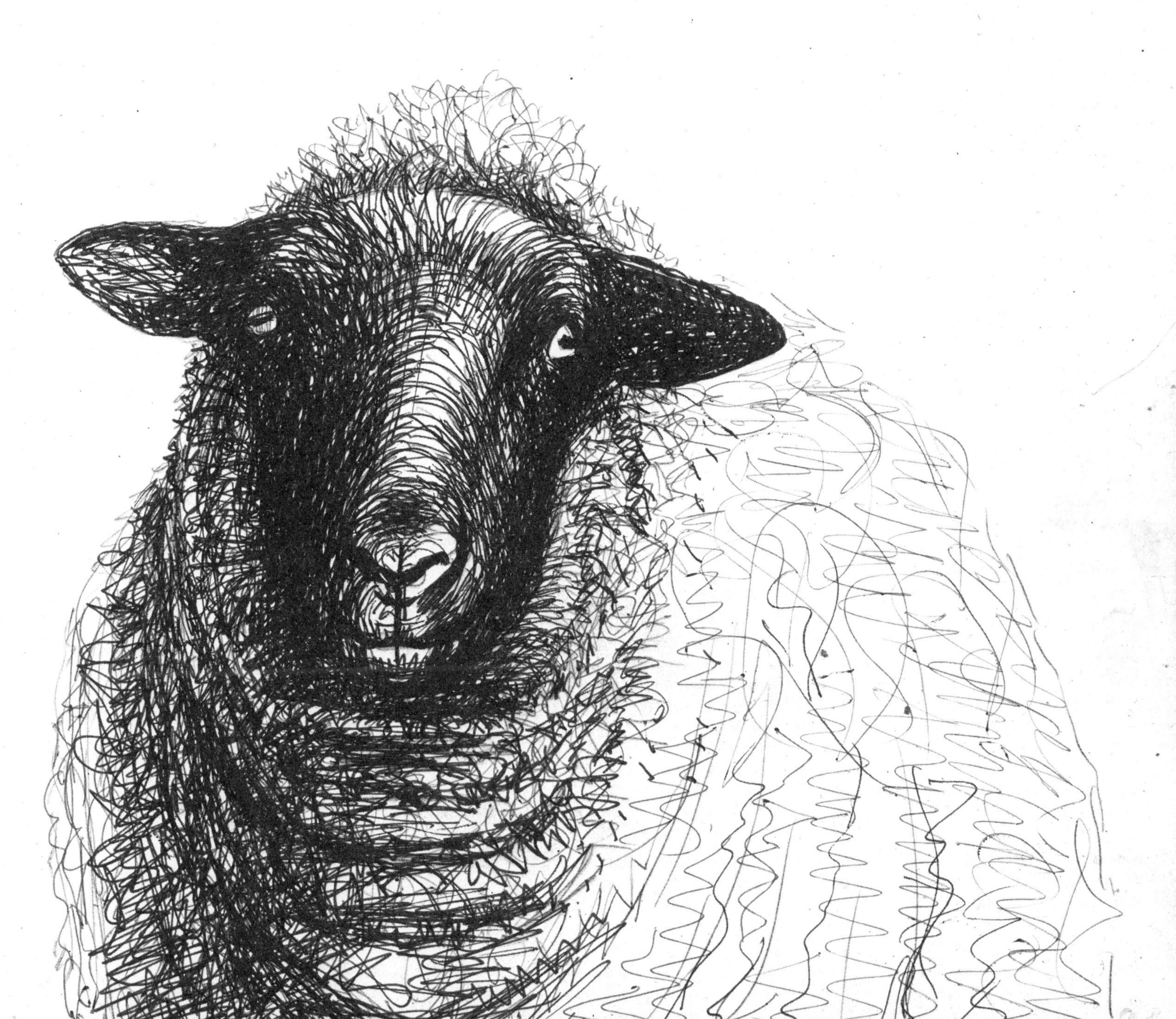

Shorn-sheets.

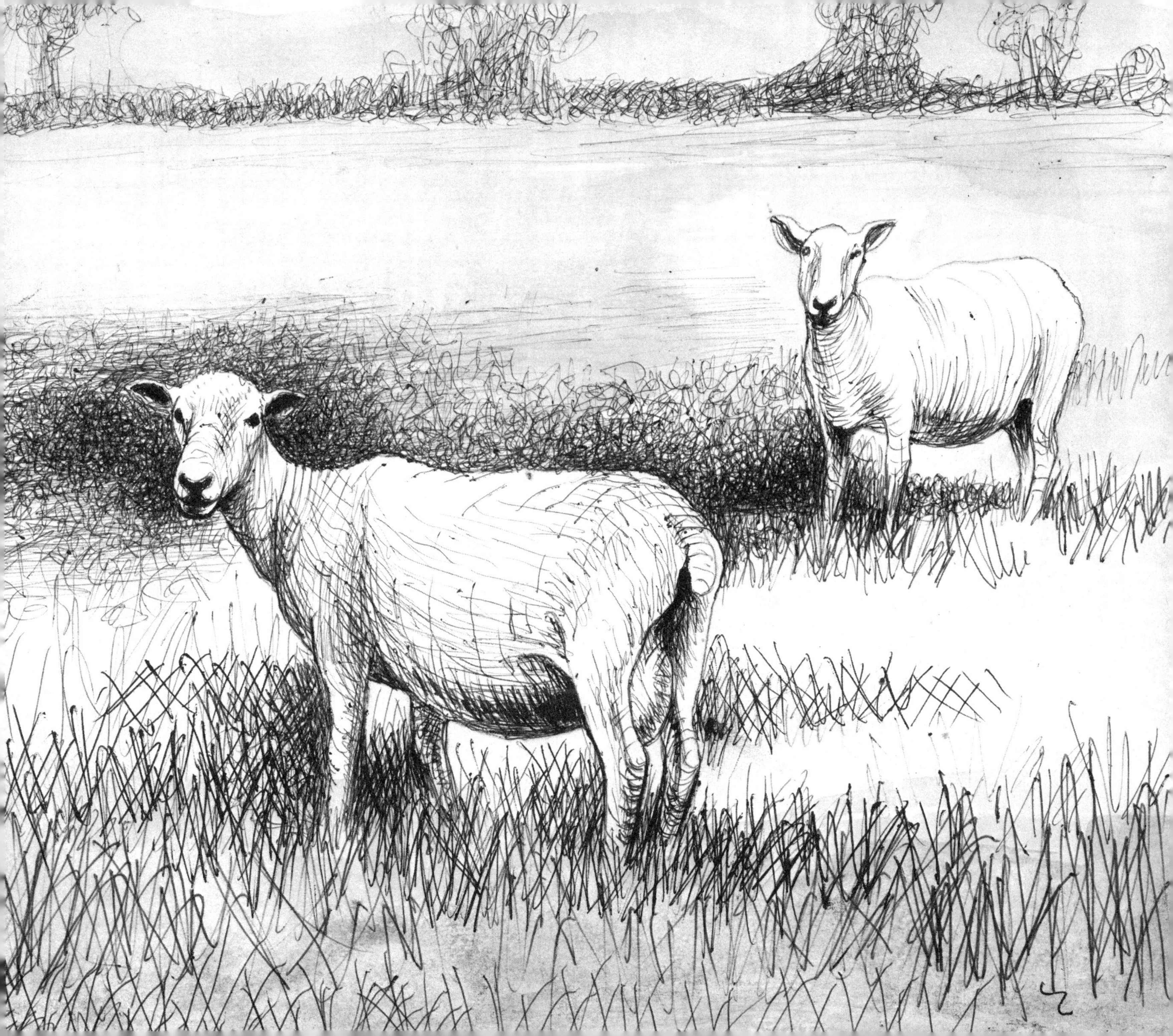

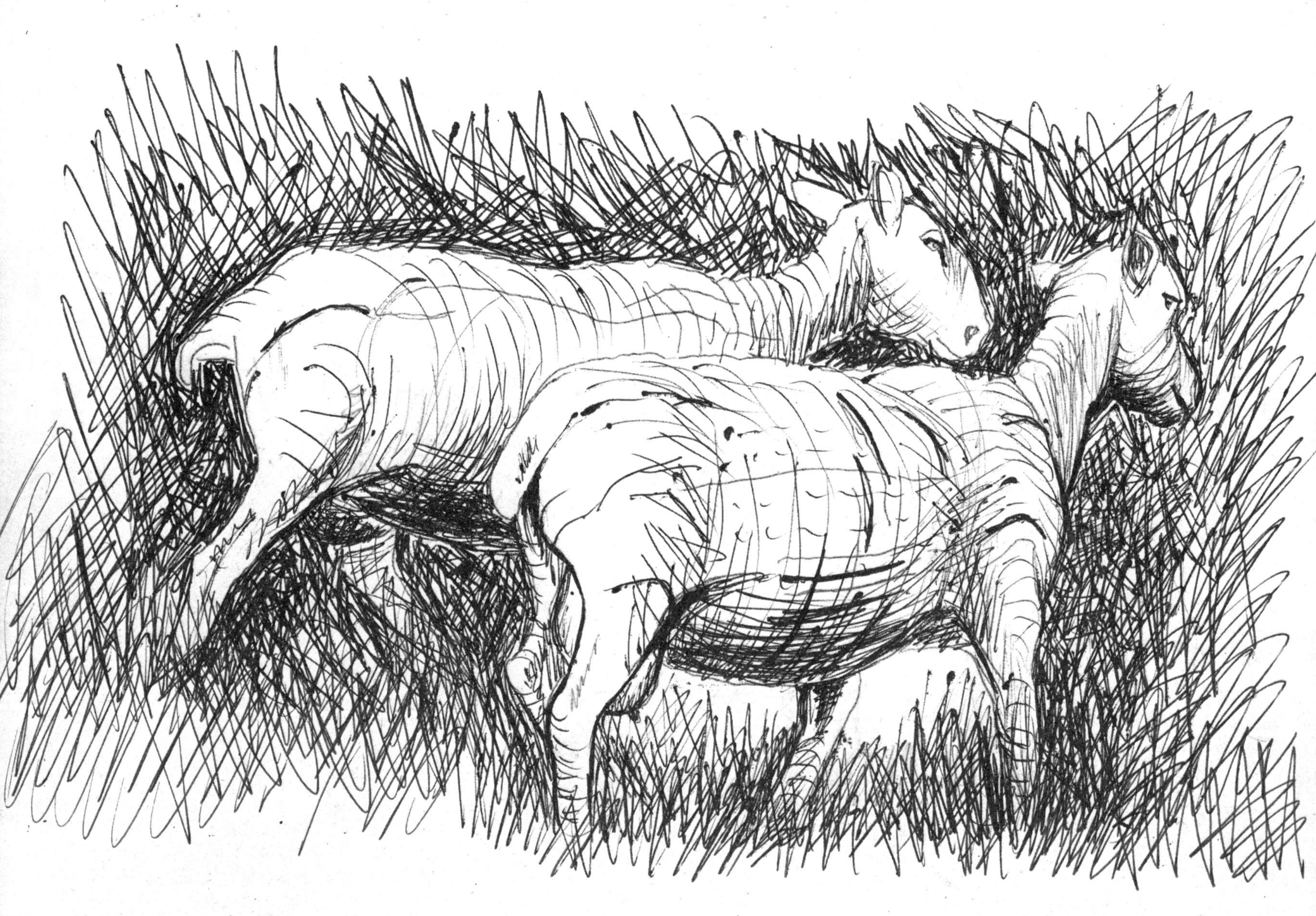

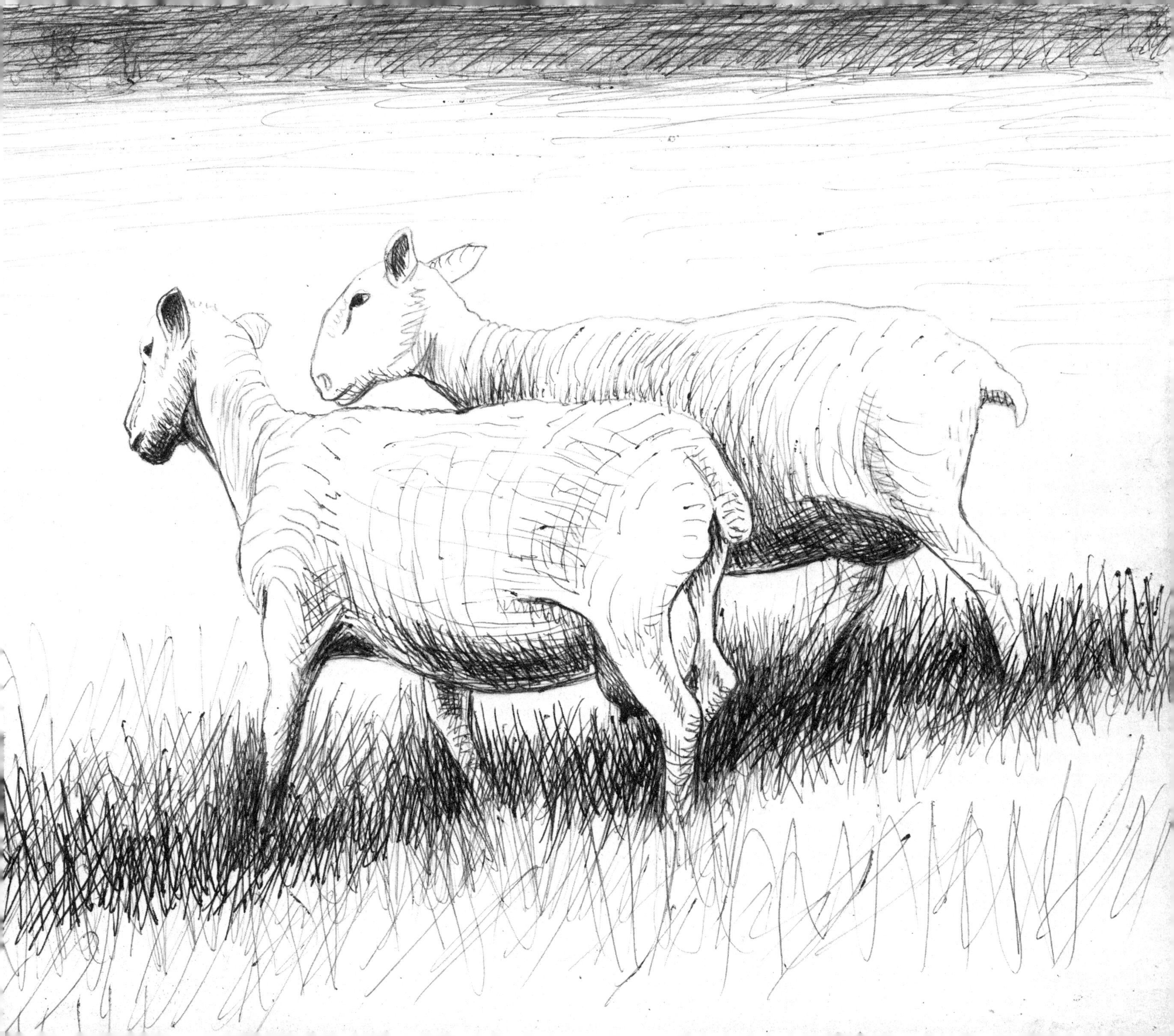

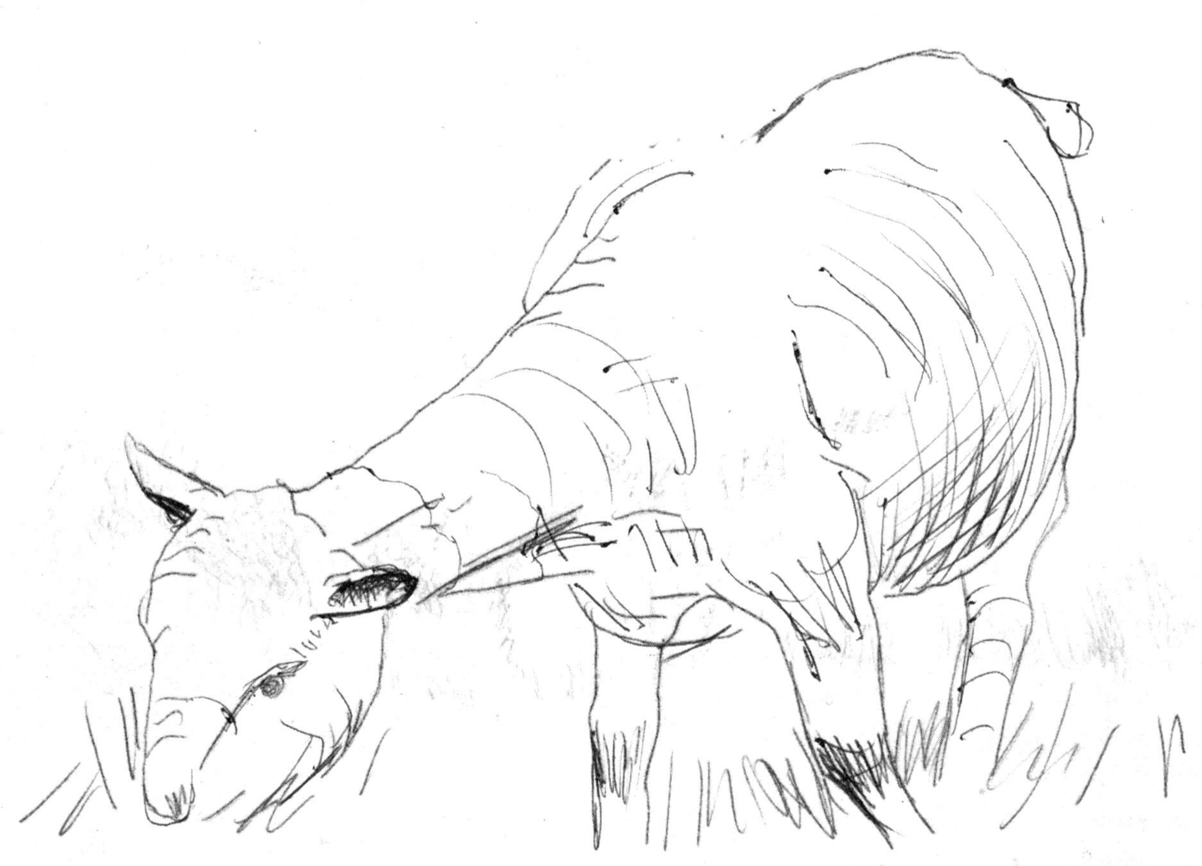

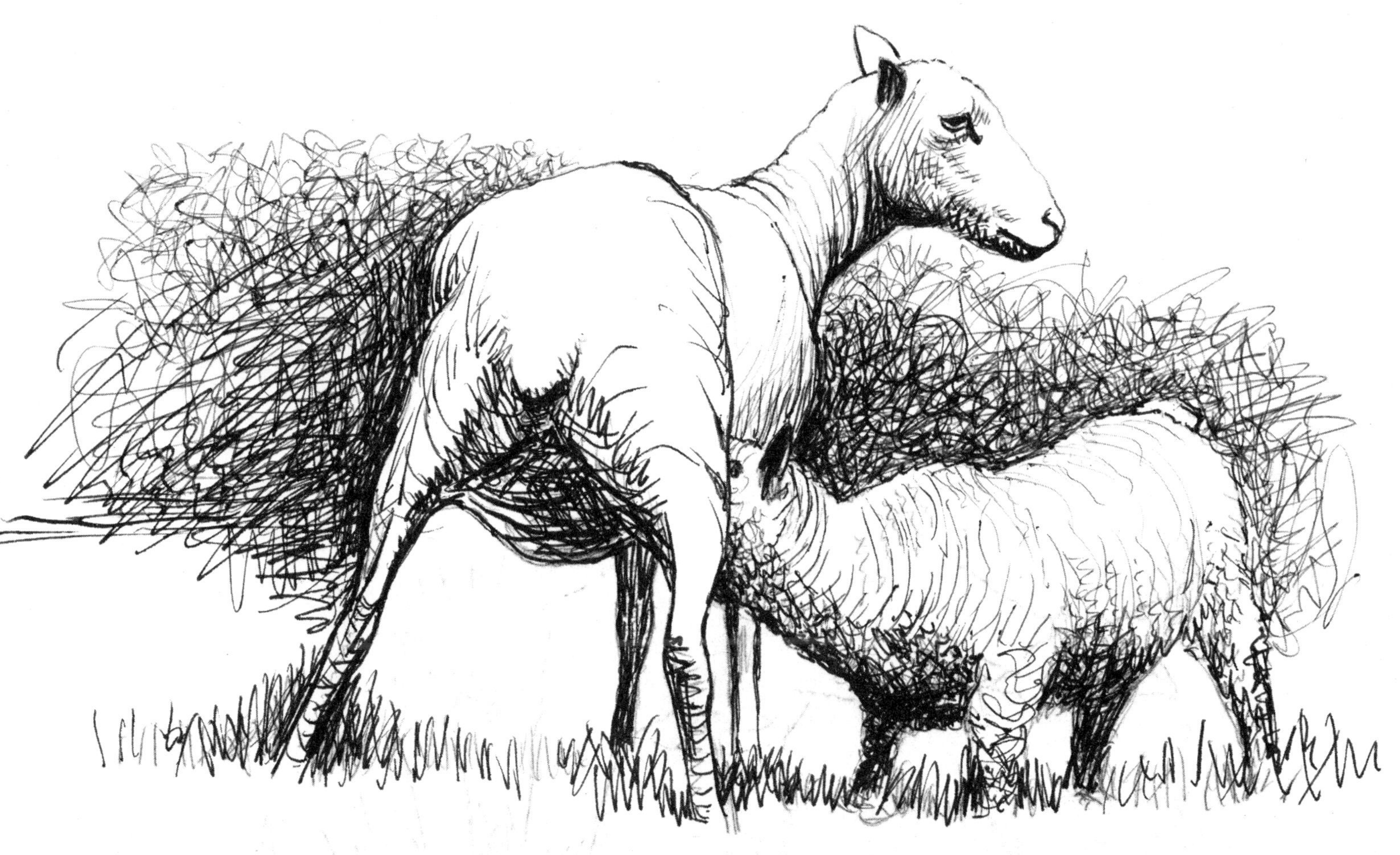

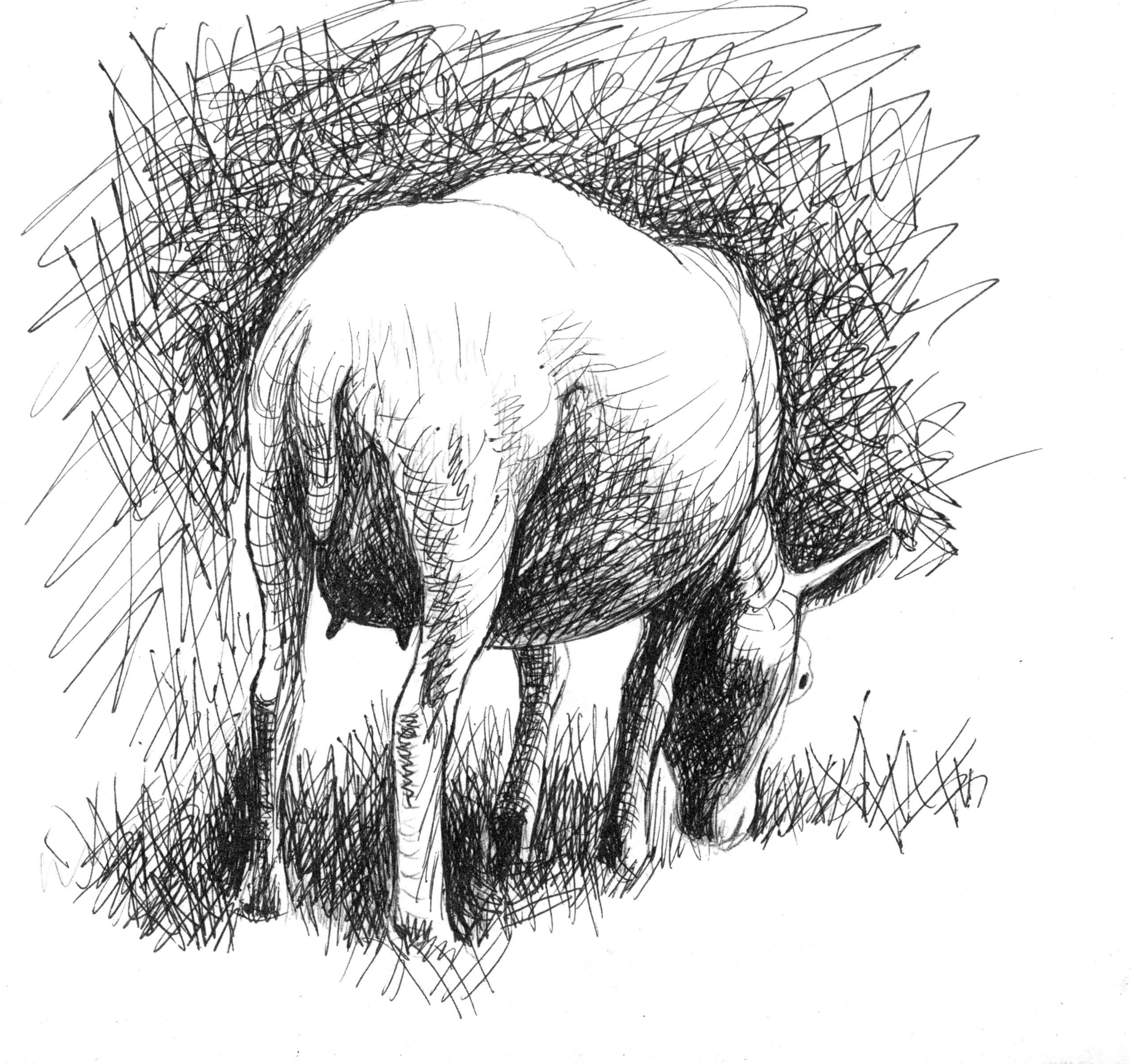

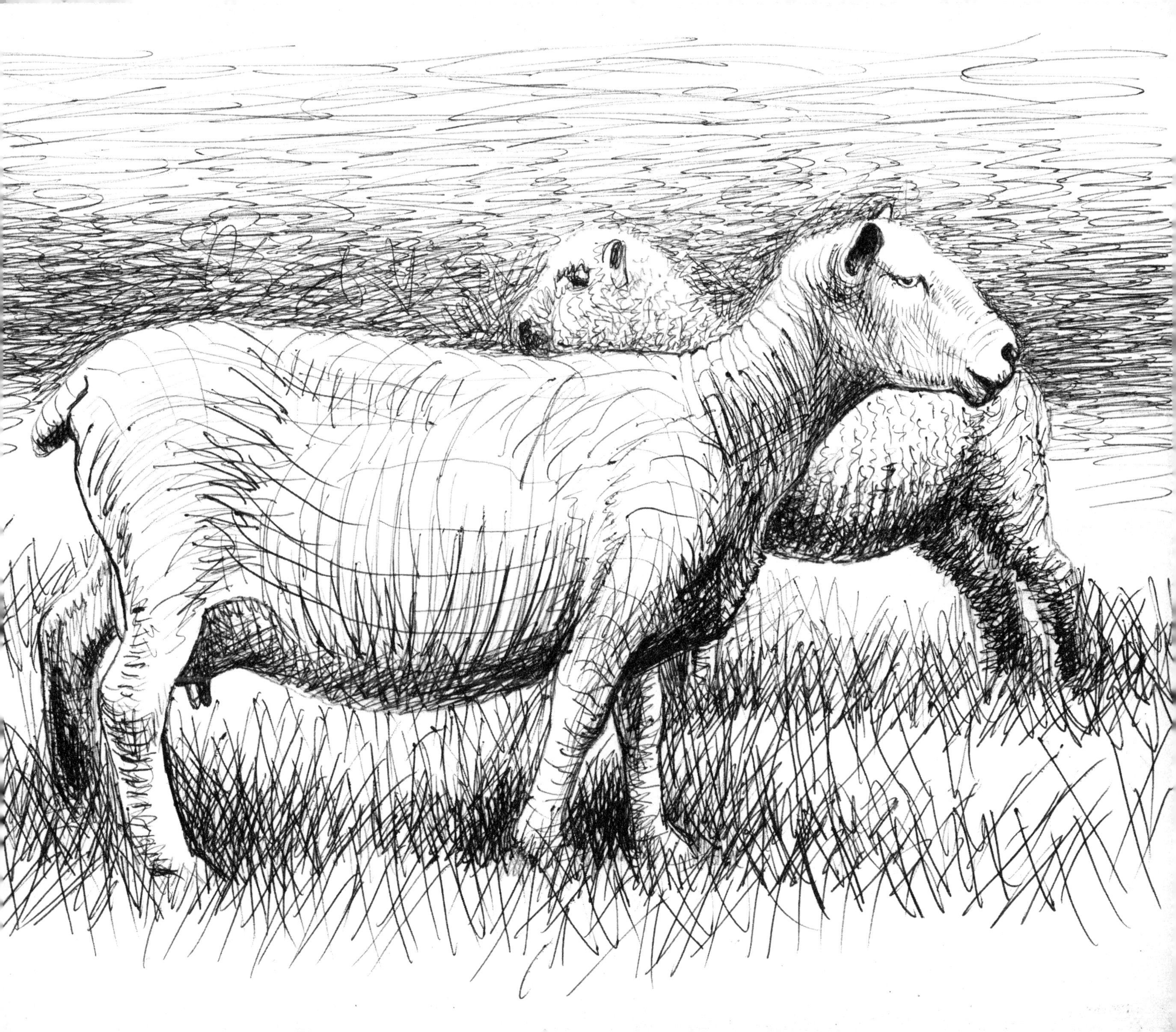

[Inside cover]

[Outside cover]

I like to imagine the feelings of an earnest Continental admirer of Henry Moore on hearing that he had devoted a fifty-page sketchbook to sheep. The English are really too puzzling. What could the master of pure form find in the shapeless bodies of these woolly animals? The answer is that a great artist can look without prejudice. We have a preconceived notion about sheep, based not only on their appearance, but on an association of ideas. This sketchbook shows that, as formal material, sheep can provide an astonishing range and variety.

To some extent Henry Moore's concentration on sheep is accidental. In the country he lives surrounded by fields full of sheep. They confront him as he goes to his work. They are the first living things he sees in the day. Although he has done many great drawings that appear to be abstractions, in fact almost all of them have been inspired by a direct visual impression. His sense of form needs continual nourishment from experience. During the greater part of the year, when he is in his home in Hertfordshire, sheep have provided his most frequent visual experience. He walks down to his studio in the morning – there are the sheep to greet him; for two hours he hammers away at some huge stone reclining figure, and then goes out for a cup of coffee. There are the sheep, still looking at him. No wonder they became a visual obsession.

Turning over the pages of this book one is astonished to find how many interesting constructions of form a ewe and lamb can produce, and how monumental a single sheep can become. We expect Henry Moore to give a certain nobility to everything he draws; but more surprising is the way in which these drawings express a feeling of real affection for their subject. It is no exaggeration to say that many of his sheep are drawn with love.

They are also drawn with consummate skill. On many pages Moore has used his pen as if it were a brush. But we do not think of the brilliant technique. We think only of the sheep, and we grow to have an affection for them almost equal to that of Moore himself.

KENNETH CLARK

I am not a purely abstract artist, and I have never tried to be. I have three or four unending themes, and the basis of all my work is the human figure. A sculpture of mine has to have a top and bottom, a head and body. It might seem to some people to be abstract, but I know which part is the head, which part is an arm, which part is a child. Animals also have something of the same human quality. They have heads, bodies and legs, and even trees remind me of human beings. All artists have some subjects that excite them more than others, and the sheep became one of those obsessive subjects.

From the earliest time I can remember, drawing was the activity I enjoyed most. I remember at my ordinary elementary school, the drawing lesson used to come on a Friday afternoon, in the last half-hour, when the teacher was tired and pleased to be off for the week-end. I loved it, not because it was the end of the week but because it was a drawing lesson. Later in my life, when I knew I wanted to be a sculptor, I realized that all the sculptors I admired from the past were great draughtsmen: Michelangelo, Bernini, Rodin. Drawing itself is a part of learning: learning to use one's eyes to see more intensely. To encourage everybody to draw is not to turn people into artists, just as you don't teach grammar to turn them all into Shakespeares. If every man were made to draw his wife, you might have a few divorces come about, but that husband would start to look more intensely at his wife and he would know much more about her. He might make a very bad drawing, but that wouldn't be the point.

My drawings of sheep began during the preparations in my studios for the big exhibition in Florence in 1972. The shippers and packers were all around, making such a disturbance that it was impossible to work, and I retired into a small studio which faces the field that I let to a local farmer for sheep grazing. I sat in this little studio making small plaster models or maquettes – I work differently now from the way I did as a young sculptor, and I now make maquettes in the round which I can imagine any size I like, but which I can hold in my hand and look at from any point of view.

I have always liked sheep, and there is one big sculpture of mine that I call *Sheep Piece* because I placed it in a field and the sheep enjoyed it and the lambs played around it. Sheep are just the right size for the kind of landscape setting that I like for my sculptures: a horse or a cow would reduce the sense of monumentality. Perhaps the sheep belong also to the landscape of my boyhood in Yorkshire. If the farmer didn't keep his sheep here, I would own some myself, just for the pleasure they give me.

These sheep often wandered up close to the window of the little studio I was working in. I began to be fascinated by them, and to draw them. At first I saw them as rather shapeless balls of wool with a head and four legs. Then I began to realize that underneath all that wool was a body, which moved in its own way, and that each sheep had its individual character. If I tapped on the window the sheep would stop and look, with that sheepish stare of curiosity. They would stand like that for up to five minutes, and I could get them to hold the same pose for longer by just tapping again on the window. It wouldn't last as long the second time, but altogether the sheep posed as well as a life model in an art school. Later I started to add settings, trying to make a pictorial arrangement. As I began to understand more about sheep, I could sometimes do further drawings in the evening from memory, or make a more finished drawing out of a rough sketch.

The packing for Italy took about three weeks, so the first twenty or thirty pages were probably done then; but I went on drawing, because the lambing season had begun, and there in front of me was the mother-and-child theme. This is one of the favourite themes in my work: the large form related to the small form and protecting it, or the complete dependence of the small form on the large form. I tried to express the way the lambs suckled with real energy and violence. There is something biblical about sheep. You don't hear of horses and cows in the Bible in the same way; you hear of sheep and shepherds.

The technique is pen drawing, done with a ballpoint. There's no real difference between using a ballpoint and another kind of pen; the important thing is that you can make a blacker line by pressing harder. Later, in turning the pages of the sketchbook, I might want to emphasize certain points, and to do this I used a black felt pen. On some pages I used a grey watercolour wash to give a softer sense of distance. When I add colour – as I did in several of these drawings – I may do it for some effect of drawing rather than for an explanation of the subject.

The large back view of a sheep on page 27 was meant to be the end of the sketchbook – like the end of a Charlie Chaplin film, where he turns his back and walks off. But I was still enjoying my sheep drawing, and so I went on with it. Later, when I came back from the Florence exhibition, and from carving in Italy through the summer, I found that the sheep had been shorn. They looked pathetically forlorn, naked, skinny, but shearing revealed the shape underneath the wool. I didn't like them as much when they were shorn. They must feel miserable; they certainly look it. So after a few more drawings of them in their shorn state, other interests took my attention, and the sketchbook ends.

HENRY MOORE

DESCRIPTION

The book consists of ten 8-page signatures. The first six signatures and two pages of the seventh are filled with drawings. The rest of the book is blank. The pages are numbered in pencil on the verso of each leaf in the top right corner. The book measures $8\frac{1}{4} \times 9\frac{7}{8}$ inches (21×25.1 cm). The front and back paper covers are reproduced here before and after the 50 drawn pages.

Cover   Ballpoint.

1 recto   Dedication. Pencil.

2 recto   Subjects. Pen and black ink, the word *Sheep* in blue ballpoint.

3   Missing (the sheet of six reclining figures was removed by the artist and is in a private collection).

4 recto   Blue-black and red ballpoint. Grey-brown wash. White gouache.

5 recto   idem.

6 recto   idem.

7 recto   idem.

8 recto   Blue-black ballpoint with pale wash.

9 recto   idem.

10 recto   idem.

11 recto   idem without wash.

12 recto   idem slight wash.

13 recto   idem slight wash.

14 recto   idem with wash.

15 recto   Blue-black and blue ballpoint with wash.

16 recto   Blue-black ballpoint.

17 recto   idem.

18 recto   idem.

19 recto   idem.

20 recto   idem.

21 recto   idem.

22 recto   idem.

23 recto   idem with pale grey wash.

24 recto   idem without wash.

25 recto   idem.

26 recto   idem with pale grey wash.

27 recto   Blue-black ballpoint. Grey wash (filling in blank area at right).

28 recto   Blue-black ballpoint.

29 recto   idem.

30 recto   idem.

31 recto   idem with blue-black felt pen.

32 recto   idem with felt pen.

32 verso   Blue-black ballpoint over felt pen bleed-through.

33 recto   Blue-black ballpoint with felt pen.

33 verso   As 32 verso.

34 recto   Blue-black ballpoint with felt pen.

34 verso   As 32 verso.

35 recto   Blue-black ballpoint. Brown wash.

36 recto   Blue-black ballpoint.

37 recto   idem with felt pen.

37 verso   idem.

38 recto   idem.

39 recto   Blue-black ballpoint.

40 recto   Blue-black ballpoint, pencil shading at top of sheet.

41 recto   Blue-black ballpoint and felt pen.

42 recto   Blue-black ballpoint and felt pen.

43 recto   Blue-black ballpoint and felt pen.

44 recto   Blue-black ballpoint and felt pen, light pencil.

45 recto   Blue-black ballpoint.

45 verso   Blue-black ballpoint scribbles with *Shorn sheep* in pencil.

46 recto   Blue-black ballpoint, pale brownish wash.

46 verso   Blue-black ballpoint.

47 recto   Blue-black ballpoint, pencil shading at top.

47 verso   Blue-black ballpoint.

48 recto   idem.

49 recto   idem.

50 recto   idem.

The artist based a number of etchings and lithographs on these studies of sheep, including an album published in 1974 which contained the six etchings made in 1972 (CGM 196-201) together with a number of additional etchings, some with aquatint (CGM 225-235).

First published in the United Kingdom in 1980 by
Thames & Hudson Ltd, 6–24 Britannia Street,
London WC1X 9JD

First published in the United States of America in 1980 by
Thames & Hudson Inc., 500 Fifth Avenue, New York,
New York 10110

EU Authorized Representative: Interart S.A.R.L.
19 rue Charles Auray, 93500 Pantin, Paris, France
productsafety@thameshudson.co.uk
interart.fr

A CIP catalogue record for this book is available from
the British Library

Library of Congress Control Number 80050325

ISBN 978-0-500-28072-0
16

Printed and bound in China by Midas Printing Ltd